Growing Up Mennonite in Puerto Rico: Nuestras Memorias

Edited by Rafael Falcón and Tom Lehman

Editorial F/L

2017

Colección Menohispana

Titles in the *Colección Menohispana* series are available at Amazon.com. Profits from sales of these books are donated to Academia Menonita Betania.

ISBN: 1544121962
ISBN-13: 978-1544121963

CONTENTS

DEDICATION

To all North Americans and Puerto Ricans whose lives have been enriched by the experience of growing up Mennonite in Puerto Rico.

ACKNOWLEDGMENTS

We want to thank Christine Yoder Falcón for her collaborative work with us. Her creative ideas, continuous energy and inspiration, and sustaining passion for our projects have made this book, like others in our Colección Menohispana, a reality. We couldn't have done it without her.

Also, our appreciation goes to Bryan Rafael Falcón for his help in designing the book cover, and for his enthusiasm and support for this project.

Finally, we want to recognize Mary Lehman's valuable role of bringing a critical eye and design sense to these books.

PREFACE

Rafael Falcón

I grew up Mennonite on the island of Puerto Rico during the decades of the 1950s and 1960s, a time during which many Puerto Ricans were still being introduced to *menonitismo* and its impact on their community. The *americanos*, who started it all, had come in 1943 to La Plata, a *barrio* in the mountainous center of the Island, to help bring about needed medical, social, educational, and economical changes to the area. Starting small, the fruits of that effort grew exponentially, leading during my growing-up years to the Hospital General Menonita de Aibonito, two denominational schools, a broadcasting network, numerous congregations, as well as other church-run programs.

In those earlier years of this Mennonite presence when I identified myself as Mennonite, the reaction on occasions was one of confusion, surprise, or even sarcasm. "You are what?," they would say. "Catholic, Baptist, or Methodist, those we know, but *menonita*?" This identification undeniably set my family and me apart. We were "different" from many of our neighborhood friends, our relatives, even the majority of the people from town with whom my father did business. Yet, being Mennonite gave me the wealth of a community in which I was a valued participant. My home congregations in La Plata and Aibonito, and my school, the Academia Menonita Betania, contributed as well, offering me a plethora of activities and companions.

In those settings of church and school my friends came from a variety of backgrounds. Some of us were Puerto Rican coming from Spanish-speaking homes, while others of us had parents who were English-speaking Mennonites from the United States and Canada. That fact did not seem to bother us though, we were all too busy experiencing life together, having fun, and creating memories. Unknown to us at that time, we were developing a rich storehouse for our future storytelling moments.

And so it happened. As I matured into adulthood, I found that whenever I encountered any of these companions of my childhood, the stories flowed. We would entertain each other with tales and vignettes we loved to recall and tell about ourselves and about each other. Intrigued by this storytelling of years gone by, I developed a yearning, a curiosity. I knew my own story of growing up on this Caribbean island, supported and surrounded by the culture of *menonitismo puertorriqueño*, and I wanted to hear the stories and reflections of others who experienced a similar reality. So, putting this inquisitiveness into action, I sent out an invitation.

It has been a success. Twelve individuals responded, interested in sharing their stories, and Galen Greaser, a good childhood friend, agreed to write the epilogue. In addition, the timeframe of the participants' stories enhanced the collection: contributors described life from the 1940s up into the 1970s. Each contribution was written in the language of the writer's preference—English or Spanish. As you will see, the majority chose to tell their stories in English.

Whatever your background, we are certain you will be delighted with these stories. Should you come to the book with a specific interest in viewing children growing up in a minority religious community within a broader Spanish-speaking culture, you will be satisfied. Should you pick up this book because a family member or friend is a writer or is mentioned in its pages, expect to be entertained. But if you happen to be one of those children who grew up Mennonite in Puerto Rico during the years of these writers, you will deeply relish reentering that world of people, places and events of an almost-forgotten childhood and adolescence. Please turn to the next page. *¡Disfruten!*

Chapter 1

LANTERN-LIGHT SERVICES
AND OTHER STORIES

Weldon Troyer

Soon after the open-sided "Tabernacle" was built in Pulguillas, a vacation Bible School was announced. We had classes for grades one through six. I was a young teenager, maybe 12 or 13 years old. My mother, Kathryn Troyer, was the teacher for first grade, and I was her helper. This entailed setting up chairs, tables, and some visual aids each day. I was also supposed to help in maintaining order while she was teaching the children, and assist the children with papers, coloring materials, and such like.

We had about 12 or 15 eager, wriggling children, boys and girls, in our little room. There was one young boy, whose name was Aníbal, who was a particularly active child, and a real handful to control. He was loud, boisterous, and hardly able to sit still for more than a few seconds at a time. Today, he would probably be labeled as having attention deficit disorder, but back then he was just disruptive. During those times when my mother was telling a Bible story or giving instructions about coloring a picture, it was hard to keep the rest of the class interested and occupied with him talking and walking around. My memory of that time is how kind and gentle my mother was with Aníbal, as she tried to find a way to teach while dealing with him.

The week of Bible school ended. At the end of the final program, I remember how proud Aníbal was with the Bible pictures and coloring papers he was given. I don't remember if we ever saw him again at the church, but my hope was that he was able to take with him a good memory of the stories and the kindness he received during that week of Bible school.

Going out Two by Two to Witness for the Lord

Soon after Lester Hershey came to La Plata to pastor the early congregation there, he organized the young people of the church to go out into the community, usually on a Sunday afternoon, to visit homes in the area. We were given the names of some suggested homes. We went out in small groups of two or three for this visitation.

When we would arrive at a house, we were instructed to ask politely if it would be alright to enter the home and share Scripture reading and prayer. After some conversation, one of us would read a previously selected scripture passage, and perhaps make some comments on what had been read. Sometimes someone in the home had questions about what had been read, and further clarifications and comments would be made. Then one of the others in the group would offer a short prayer and blessing for the persons in the home. After that we would walk on to the next destination, and repeat the visit. Usually we were assigned to three or four homes on a particular afternoon.

I still have a vivid memory of one visit when we were asked to leave a home and never come back. A young Catholic seminarian had recently come to La Plata and had been in conversation with Lester. He had started to have serious doubts about some of the teachings of the Catholic Church, and had decided to leave the seminary to explore other religious beliefs. The scripture had been read, and the seminarian was commenting on the passage, when the husband of the home, who had been in an adjoining room suddenly stormed into the room where we were and began to berate and curse the seminarian. He said, "These other boys are all Mennonites, and don't know any better, but you have studied in a Catholic seminary and should of all people know better than to spread these lies! Get out of this house, and never come back."

A hurried prayer from one of us followed, and we got up and left the home. The mother of the house walked with us out to the road and apologized for her husband's words and action. We reassured her of our desire to not further anger her husband, and thanked her again for allowing us to enter their home.

Easter Sunrise Service

In the early morning predawn light, we walked in single file over a hill and down a few hundred feet to a small flat *meseta* overlooking the descending foothills to the plains and south coast of Puerto Rico. It was Easter morning in March, and the air was chilly. All of us were wearing warm coats, and some had hats. A few early shafts of sunlight touched the scene before us as the sun was just rising into a beautiful azure blue sky. Our group of about fifteen youth and our pastor stood in a circle while we sang *coritos* and heard again the old, but ever new, story of that first Easter morning at the tomb near Jerusalem. When the sun had risen over the hill behind us, and our group was bathed in bright light, we returned to the church building in Pulguillas to warm up with hot chocolate and conversation, and to await the regular morning worship service. A beautiful way to celebrate, once again, the wonderful Resurrection story!

A *Gira* to the Beach

Every so often the youth of the church, along with the leaders and mentors, would plan a trip to the beach. Since we lived in the center of the Island, we would have to find transportation, (usually an open truck with side rails), and then make all the plans for destination, food and drink, and the necessary permissions. We would usually plan for at least an hour or more for travel, depending on how far the beach was from the church.

One Saturday we went to the beach at Guánica, a town on the south coast of the Island. We were about 15 or 20 young men and women, and we all piled into the truck. There were no seats, just places to stand and hang on the railings on the side of the truck. Of course, there were no seat belts! It was not the safest way to travel, but in that day it didn't matter, since everyone traveled that way.

On arriving at the beach, which had no amenities such as changing rooms or tables, the boys went one way into the forest to change and the girls went the other way. Then, we were free to walk down the beach to search for shells, or to swim out to where the waves were breaking. One had to watch for hazards, such as spiny sea urchins and sharp rocks, and we were advised to always go with a companion or two, so that we could help each other in case of an accident or sudden need for assistance.

At noon we all gathered back at the truck for lunch, and then were advised to not return to swimming for at least a half hour while we digested the food. Persons with lighter skin color were strongly advised to apply plenty of sunscreen because at midday in the tropics the sun was bright and hot, and a painful sunburn could quickly sneak up on you.

About four o'clock in the afternoon we were all tired and ready to climb back into the truck for the trip home. We were all sticky from the salt water, and there was no fresh water to rinse or shower in. So we all pulled on our clothes, got in the truck, and headed up the long road to the central mountains. Conversation was usually much more subdued on the way home, since everyone was tired and ready for a nap.

On returning to the church, which we had left in the morning, some of the youth still had to walk some distance to their homes, which could be several miles away. But we all had good memories of fun and comradeship during the trip to sustain us.

Boys Camp Memories

In the late 1940s and early 1950s, I attended several annual boys' camps, which were sponsored and staffed by the Mennonite Church. The first one I remember was at a Methodist camp on the road between Comerío and Bayamón called "McClain's". There were about 40 or 50 campers in all. The camp had sleeping facilities and a large dining room with kitchen, and was located in a beautiful rural setting.

The usual day began with wake-up at 6 a.m., followed by morning devotions and breakfast. During the day there were many activities planned, such as crafts, Bible study, and clean up. After the noon meal, there was often a trip to a nearby sports area, where we could organize softball games, basketball, and other physical activities. I remember running in a one-kilometer road race with five other boys. There was a small prize for the winner.

In the evening there was always a time when we would gather for an inspirational program of singing, praise and adoration, and testimonies. Afterward there was some brief free time before lights-out came at 10 o'clock. There were plenty of practical jokes, and other high jinks, which made these times of togetherness special to the campers.

I attended these camps both as a camper, and later on, as a counselor. Subsequent camping events were located at a YMCA site in the Luquillo rainforest, which was a fun place to go. It had a much more backwoods feel, and there was a clear, cold mountain stream running through it, where we would go to swim during the afternoons. This camp was a favorite place to go during the warm summer months after school was over for the year.

Many of the youth made commitments to Jesus Christ during these camps, and remember them as the place where they made a new beginning in their lives.

Baptist Academy of Barranquitas: High School in the Mountains

When I was 13 years old, I started high school studies at the Baptist Academy of Barranquitas (BAB). At that time our family lived in Pulguillas, so my parents had to take me to the school on Sunday afternoon. I stayed at the boarding school all week, returning by public transportation on Friday afternoon after classes were finished. At that time, Stanley Miller was the principal of BAB, and several Mennonite personnel from the La Plata Service Unit were working there as teachers and staff. One of the missionary children, Fred Springer, was also a student at BAB.

Although I already knew some Spanish, I soon was learning a lot of new words as we studied science, history, math, social studies, and Spanish grammar, all in a new language. Living in a dormitory with other students also provided plenty of opportunity to use conversational Spanish. All students, male and female, had to donate one hour a day by working at the school. For the boys, that usually meant working in the large garden that the school maintained to supply food for the dining hall. However, sometimes the work would be cleaning classrooms or helping in the kitchen.

Some of the students were from nearby Barranquitas, and were not boarding at the Academy. Others were recently released veterans from World War II, who were taking advantage of the opportunity to study and obtain their high school diploma through the GI Program. Since they were older and more mature, they were frequently used as supervisors of the younger boarding students.

There were many activities that were available to us. Sports were intramural: we had softball, track and field, and volleyball. Ping pong competitions were set up, and many students took part in them.

Boarding students were strongly encouraged to attend Sunday evening worship services at the small Baptist church in Barranquitas. I was able to attend about half the time. There was no youth group in the church, and very few youth who attended from the congregation.

One year we had a small choir at school, led by Miss Carol Glick, one of the BAB staff. Before the annual Baptist conference meeting, she picked out four young men from the choir, and asked us to prepare several well-known hymns to sing at the conference. I still remember going to the town of Carolina, and standing before—what seemed to me—a huge audience to sing three quartet numbers.

After studying at BAB for three years, I had completed all the scholastic requirements for graduation, except for one credit hour. My counselor, Miss Glick, strongly advised me to consider leaving the high school and enrolling at Hesston College in Hesston, Kansas, for the next school year. At that time Hesston Academy and College was credentialed as both a high school and a junior college, so I could complete the one credit needed for high school graduation, and take a full freshman college program in the same year. After discussing the opportunity with my parents, we decided to make that change and in the late summer of 1949, I went to Kansas to continue my education. I missed my many friends at BAB, but soon made new ones in Kansas.

Assisting with Clinics in Rabanal and Coamo Arriba

After completing college in 1953, I returned to Puerto Rico to work at the La Plata Mennonite Hospital as a I-W to satisfy the government service requirement for conscientious objectors. My job in the hospital was as a laboratory technician, but I also volunteered for work in the outlying clinics of Rabanal de Cidra and Coamo Arriba. The work at these clinics involved helping the doctor and nurse care for the patients who showed up, and also to assist in any way with the religious services that usually followed the clinics.

Since there were no roads to either place, only mountainous dirt paths, we had to ride there and back on horseback, or walk. Another I-W fellow and I would start out from La Plata after regular hospital hours were over, about 5 o'clock in the evening, and catch and saddle two horses for the trip. After following the trail along the La Plata River for about 25 minutes, we would arrive at a ford that was a relatively shallow place. There was no bridge either way for at least 10 miles. After crossing the river, trying to keep our feet dry, we would begin the uphill segment of the trail, which could take another 45 to 60 minutes.

Going up to the Rabanal clinic was relatively easy, as it was still daylight. When we came back down at 9 or 10 o'clock at night, though, it was usually pitch dark, and we had to rely completely on the ability of the horses to navigate the steep, narrow path. There were always two or three gates we had to pass through, coming and going, and it was not acceptable to leave a gate open, because other animals could then go through them and get lost.

One memorable evening when we finished clinic and returned down the mountain, we got to the ford, and found that rain upstream in the mountains had caused the river to rise considerably. My companion and I discussed what we should do since the river had risen by several feet, and was faster and much more forceful. It was already past 10 p.m., and if we didn't cross, we had nowhere to stay overnight. There was no moon, and the dark night was impenetrable.

We finally decided to try the crossing, and went into the river together. We soon realized that both horses were swimming, and that we were being swept downstream. Fortunately, we landed safely on the other side, both soaked from the waist down, but glad that we were over the river safely. "Thank you Jesus!" When we got home to the CPS unit, we unsaddled the horses, gave them grain to eat, and headed wearily back to the bunkhouse to dry out.

The trip from Pulguillas down to Coamo Arriba was not as perilous as the trail from La Plata up to Rabanal, but it was just as steep. It usually would take about an hour to travel down, but would be more like an hour and fifteen minutes to climb back up on the return. The horses were usually loaded with all kinds of supplies, so sometimes we had to get off and walk alongside them while they climbed the hill back to Pulguillas. At times, we would even hang onto the horses' tails, (*guindarse al anca*), to help us get back up the hill again.

I still have a vivid memory of the lantern-light services; the simple, but sincere gospel messages; and the gratitude seen in the eyes of the *campesinos* for the health care and worship that had been shared with them.

Helping to Plant a New Church

In 1957 I was studying medicine in San Juan, and newly married to my wife, Frances. We lived in a small upstairs apartment in Santurce, and to make a little extra money I was working as a receptionist at Robert Ehret's funeral home in Hato Rey on weekends.

Don Bernadino and Doña Ramona Miranda, who with their family of twelve children had been attending the Palo Hincado Mennonite Church near Barranquitas for several years, had recently moved to the metropolitan area for better work opportunities. His brother Juan Miranda and family also lived in the metropolitan area. They wanted to have a Mennonite church home in the metro area, but couldn't find one that was nearby. When Robert Ehret heard about their need, he graciously offered space for meetings in a casket room on the second floor of his funeral home.

Soon I was recruited to drive to the Miranda home in Bayamón, in a vehicle supplied by Bob Ehret, to pick up members of the family and bring them to Hato Rey on Sunday mornings.

My parents, Dr. George and Kathryn Troyer, would drive to Hato Rey on Sunday mornings to assist with the services in the casket room. George would preach in English, and either Kathryn or I would translate into Spanish for those who needed it. Other families who would attend were my older brother Nortell and family, who were living in Río Piedras, and sometimes other Mennonite families who were living and working in the area.

This continued for several years, until a Mennonite school was built in the Summit Hills area of San Juan. Along with the school, a Mennonite church was started in 1960. In June of that year, I graduated from medical school, and moved back to the United States to serve an obligatory internship in Indianapolis. Some of the believers from Hato Rey started attending the new church in Summit Hills. In 1965, a Mennonite church was begun in Bayamón, and I believe that most, if not all of the Miranda family began to attend at that church.

From these small beginnings, the Gospel was preached in many new areas, and I was glad that our small family could be a part of this ministry.

Chapter 2

YOUTHFUL YEARS IN PUERTO RICO

Barbara Amstutz Hodel

What an adventure to anticipate! We would be going to a far-away place called Puerto Rico! We had never heard of it before our father, H. Clair Amstutz, went there as a conscientious objector (C.O.) during World War II. Being a medical doctor, his age of 38 was no excuse to avoid the draft. However, the local draft board had granted many more men C.O. status than had been allotted it, so he obtained an "Essential" classification, and went with Mennonite Central Committee (MCC) to an underserved area for which the U.S. government was responsible. Now, after a year of service there, my mother and we children could join him. There were four of us siblings: I, Barbara, was 9; my sister Vivian was 8; my brother John was 5; and the youngest, Carolyn, was almost 3.

I have since wondered how Mother handled that difficult year during Dad's absence, and the ensuing move to Puerto Rico. She was in full agreement with his motives, however, and pleased to be able to join him in service. Finally our time to go arrived. In the spring of 1945 we made a long train trip to Miami, where we boarded a plane for San Juan. Vivian and I learned that, no, it was not hotter in the plane due to its proximity to the sun, but colder because of its altitude!

Arrival in La Plata

Once we arrived in La Plata, life for me was one big adventure. I was curious by nature and took in everything with excitement. The medical center where Dad practiced medicine was a converted tobacco barn, part of a government project called Puerto Rico Reconstruction Administration (PRRA). There were a number of substantial buildings: a school, a community center, a "milk station" to feed undernourished kids, a swine project, and small concrete homes arranged in a village pattern.

The MCC Unit, as we called it, consisted of around twenty young men with Conscientious Objector status, and women from the United States. These unit members lived in several wooden houses, a bunkhouse, and a dormitory. Our family of six stayed in two rooms of that dormitory until a house was built for "the doctors' families." With our father's arrival, hospital and clinic service had expanded to two medical doctors, the senior one being Dr. George Troyer.

Childhood Curiousity and Adventures

We older children were entranced with the tropical plants and animals in that pleasantly warm climate—rarely hot due to the mountain altitude. The hilly landscape was fascinating, and we all spent a lot of time playing outdoors. There were, of course, certain restrictions for health's sake: no going barefoot because of hookworm in the unsanitary soil; no playing in the streams because of the bilharzia organisms there; no drinking of water except the purified water in our homes, and periodic checks to see if we (all of us in the unit) were infected with any internal parasites. One warning we did not hear turned out to our distress: when we were playing with our Puerto Rican friends our heads must have been too close together. The result was we had to have treatment for head lice—our long braids lopped off to make way for daily shampoos, fine-tooth combing, and kerosene application.

In that remote mountainous area of the Island, we children were objects of curiosity. Puerto Rican children would come to our screen door to peer in, to see how these *americanos* lived. Esperanza and María Elisa and their friends came to play with us, speaking Spanish of course, and teaching us their singing games. (Vivian and I can still sing those songs!)

We somehow learned Spanish. Vivian remembers she suddenly found herself conversing in the language without trying. And though we both continued classes for Spanish through high school, Vivian states that learning the language was one of the things she valued highly from her Puerto Rico experience. I must confess, we giggled at Mother's accent when we heard her using Spanish. How naturally speech is picked up by children, and how hard to learn when an adult!

School and Unit Life

When the traditional time for school came around, Mother vacated her tiny kitchen, putting in three homemade desks for the third, fourth, and eighth graders, and two chairs for the kindergarteners. So we older sisters and Weldon Troyer, the eighth-grader, were taught by Mother, whose teacher training in college came in handy. The five-year-olds were my brother John, and the boy next door who was his age, Duane Martens, son of the unit administrator.

We even had a school program at the end of the year, dutifully attended by some of our unit friends. We borrowed a tune from an old song, and made up words:

> School days, school days;
> Dear old MCC days!
> Reading and writing and 'rithmetic
> Taught to the tune of a bamboo stick
> In our eight by ten schoolroom.
> We were the problems of MCC!
> Whene'er we were pleased, we laughed and sneezed!
> When our dads worked for MCC!

We enjoyed the young men of the unit; they treated us as if we were their little brothers and sisters. The two boys of kindergarten age were often invited—perhaps self-invited!—to join one of the short trips made by the unit drivers to the barn, to town for supplies, to the cowsheds, or to other places.

We often joined the unit's socials, and especially loved the picnics at one or another of the Carribean beaches. Swimming, sand, and sunburn were fun things for most; the occasional group food poisoning was not. The kitchen crew had to learn to somehow refrigerate those potato and macaroni salads.

We children had considerable freedom, and so could observe the many aspects of the mission and work of the unit. We avoided the premises of the hospital, although we sometimes saw patients arriving, often carried in a primitive "ambulance" from over mountain trails in a hammock between two men. Some Civilian Public Service members worked in the X-ray department or the laboratory, while others were assigned to the laundry that serviced the hospital. Others worked in public health activities, like building latrines for the countryside huts that served as homes. The women were nurses in the clinic or on the wards. My mother taught the first nurse-aide classes begun at the hospital during our second year there, which necessitated our family having household help by local women. And after the first heifers from Heifer Project were sent to Puerto Rico to our unit and to the Brethren unit at Castañer, several from the unit were assigned to cattle care. We children were excited about those two new pets, naming them, and bringing them stalks of grasses to munch on.

School in Santurce

The second year in La Plata, my sister Vivian and I were sent to an English private school in Santurce. Robinson School was an English (British) boarding school, where girls were boarded through grade 12, and boys were day students up through grade six. I realized that my sister and I would have to look out for each other; we started by braiding one another's hair each morning. Vivian recalls being homesick for a few weeks, and I didn't like the food. Nevertheless I felt good at being able to rise to the challenge.

Many weekends we were able to catch a ride back to La Plata with unit members who drove the trucks to San Juan for supplies. When we stayed in Santurce, we were sometimes invited to the homes of friends of our parents. We also visited in the homes of classmates: they were students who had parents in the United States military, on the university faculty, or worked in government. People were kind. One student's mother gave me the right things to wear for the sixth grade graduation. I had not told anyone that my parents were given an allowance from MCC of only $10 a month per adult beyond maintenance expenses, but somehow that mother guessed my needs.

Broadening Experiences

Our parents made sure we had educational and family outings, too. We visited the CPS-related units of other denominations. Dad was interested in comparing medical work in other communities. We young ones were curious about the homes, landscapes, and people we met from other churches. One Sunday morning Dad took me to the US army barracks near Cayey, to hear E. Stanley Jones preach to the soldiers there.

Another cultural experience we had was evacuating our home, along with the other buildings, and moving into the Community Center because of a hurricane bearing down on the Island. Piles of mattresses, as well as food and water, were brought to the Center. As for the hospital patients, most had their families come to take them home. I found that hard to understand, since the homes were frequently flimsy buildings. Others were carried in their beds to the Center. The work of the unit stopped. I remember standing outside with some of the others, staring up at the heavy gray clouds racing across the sky from east to west—an ominous direction. I wondered what the countryside people could do in their huts on stilts to avoid the coming fury. But the hurricane passed by the island, and we went home to sleep. I must confess to a bit of disappointment in my sense of relief!

We children were neither protected from nor immersed in the culture of poverty that surrounded us in the mountains there. We saw glimpses of the suffering and deprivation of the Puerto Ricans, but we knew we were there because of our parents' goals: to ameliorate the difficulties, and hopefully show them a better way to live. The mission my parents and other MCCers were on was not so much to evangelize, but to alleviate the unhealthful effects of poverty and demonstrate loving service "in the name of Christ."

On Religion and Ethnicity

Eventually, the (then named) Mennonite Board of Missions and Charities stepped in to provide pastor Lester Hershey to the La Plata community, and a chapel was built by unit members with community assistance for the service of all the community. So there were worship services in Spanish, in which we all took part. My father made arrangements to have an old school bell brought from Ohio. It rang out Sunday mornings, announcing worship time to those who had no clocks or watches to use.

That bell rang out for weddings between unit members too! Unit life was a fitting way to get to know one another on a daily work-a-day basis. Relationships formed between the Mennonite young men and the Puerto Rican women working at the hospital as well. A few unit members had enough prejudice to frown on this. In spite of some concern over cultural differences, our father came down hard on those who criticized on the basis of different skin color.

As we children saw it, there was very little difference in status in Puerto Rico due to color. The long history of mixing of white conquerors, their black slaves, and the native *Borinqueños* had seen to that. There was a definite class distinction between rich and poor, however. The wealthy persons we knew demonstrated their financial status with a well-filled-out body build, as well as soft hands that refrained from any manual labor.

We were aware of the Catholic influence in the communities, even if there were no church nearby. We were led to respect their scruples, even to our parents forbidding our use of the phrase *"¡Ave María!"* because "it was like swearing for the Catholics," an exclamation of disgust, surprise, or such, instead of a prayer. We understood the special garb that women wore who had made a vow. We got glimpses of the church festivals in Aibonito. A highlight was the observation of Good Friday, with a magnificent parade. As for the unit's Easter celebration, we had an early service out on a mountainside, in the light of a wonderful sunrise.

Leaving La Plata

Then the war was over, and it was time for the Amstutz family to leave. The unit held a farewell supper, complete with *lechón asado*. I piled my plate high with the foods I had come to enjoy. Then came the unexpected word: the charter flight we were to take from San Juan was leaving that very night, instead of the next evening, as we had been told. Upset at having to leave precipitously, I could only stare at my plate without eating. I loved La Plata and hated to leave.

At that farewell occasion, my mother apologized to the group for the sins of her children. Then the women of the unit came to our house and helped with the final packing. It was a difficult ending, complete with a wild ride by car through the mountains to San Juan airport, and a violently stormy flight to the United States that Dad did not expect us to live through.

But we lived, and thrived on the experiences, perspectives, and understandings that God had so graciously given us through this glimpse of service "in the name of Christ." As my sister Vivian put it: it was a wonderful experience for a child, growing up in a safe family, in a bilingual setting, and imbibing a spirit of acceptance and cooperation in a place of diversity.

Chapter 3

YOU REALLY CAN GO HOME AGAIN

Sherilyn Hershey Layne

"You grew up in Puerto Rico?" "Yes," I answer with a smile. They look at me like they're not sure if they should feel sorry for me, or if maybe this could be an interesting conversation. "My parents were missionaries there for 35 years," I continue, "and I lived there 16 years." "Oh! Did you like growing up there?" Hmmm...I wonder if I should ask them how they liked growing up in Virginia, New York City, Ohio, or Oregon, all places where I've lived since leaving Puerto Rico in 1963.

A New Home in Puerto Rico

In April, 1947, my family boarded an airplane and made the first of many trips back and forth to and from Puerto Rico. My parents had served in Chicago for several years at the Mennonite Mexican Mission, and all three of us kids were born there. Now here we were—Daddy, Mother, Jan (3 1/2), me (1 1/2) and Gene (4 months)—moving to a place about which we knew very little. Mother was a farm girl-turned-teacher from Illinois, and Daddy grew up on the mission field in Argentina. Even though they were certain they were following God's call to become missionaries in a "foreign land," I'm sure they wondered at times what challenges lay ahead for us.

Our first home in Puerto Rico was in La Plata, which was also home to the I-W and Mennonite Voluntary Service (VS) unit. There was a lot of interaction between us and the VSers, and we became like family. One of the VSers was a dietician at the Hospital Menonita, and she had white mice that she used for nutrition studies. I vividly remember visiting her one time and being fascinated by these critters. I stuck my little finger in the cage, and you guessed it...I cried inconsolably!

When the three of us were a little older, but still needed a babysitter while Mother and Daddy would be away in the evenings, Ruth stayed with and taught us some really funny songs. Later when she got married she asked us to sing "There's a Big Fat Turkey Down On Grandpa's Farm" at her wedding. Oh, my!

We left La Plata and moved to Pulguillas for a while, and when we came back to La Plata there were quite a few kids from the area who were attending Betania School, about 30 minutes away. We didn't have a school bus, so a big old flatbed truck was enclosed with sides and a roof, and the back was sort of a fence to keep us from sliding out. It was left open, but had a roll-down cover in case it rained. Rows of benches were built inside from front to back, one on each side and two back-to-back, right down the middle. A drop-down gate completed the "*camioneta*." It was pretty close quarters, but we sure had fun traveling back and forth to school.

One morning I didn't finish my chores on time, and I guess my punishment was missing "the truck" to school. I never could quite figure it out, though, because then Mother had to take me in our car to catch up, which took about ten minutes since they stopped to pick up kids along the way. Lesson learned? Maybe, but I still don't like doing morning chores!

Life on Betania Hill

Some of my fondest memories were when we lived on the "Betania Hill" in Pulguillas where the school, the church, and several missionaries' homes were located. Our MK (missionary kid) friends on the Hill were Margaret and Arnie Snyder and the Greaser boys: Galen, David, and Danny. Gene and Galen would climb the big *higüera* tree in the front yard of the houses and sing at the top of their lungs. I'm not sure how many of them were involved in our plans to build an elaborate system of tunnels and underground rooms were we could hide out in case we were bombed by the Russians. We didn't dig more than a few feet into the side of the hill before giving up on the idea. Another time, Gene tried to dig a swimming pool behind the casita where Carlos and Mabel Lugo lived, but that attempt didn't fare too well either!

We had a hired girl, Guilla, when we lived at Betania. This may seem a bit presumptuous for missionaries, but Mother was almost as busy as Daddy when it came to church work, so we had help. Mother hiked up and down the hills doing visitation or Bible studies, or she worked in the office of La Hora del Calvario (The Calvary Hour), which later became Audición Luz y Verdad (Light and Truth Broadcast), that Daddy felt led to start. She also taught at Betania School for a while. Guilla cleaned our house, did the laundry and ironing, did some of the cooking, and cared for the three of us. We loved Guilla, and she really became part of our family.

Many times we'd walk the two or three miles up to Ismael Torres' store to buy a penny or two of bread and butter and a penny's worth of *bacalao* (salted dried cod fish). What a treat! One time though, when Mother and Daddy were away, we wanted to go to the store but didn't have enough money. I don't know whose bright idea it was to take a penny from the peanut can up in the kitchen cupboard, but when the folks came home they mysteriously found out about the "big robbery," and Jan and I were punished soundly. Lesson learned for sure this time!

Three gentlemen from the Betania Church always stood out in my mind, three pillars of the church, and to look at them you would wonder what in the world they had in common—Don Pepe, tall, distinguished looking, and straight as an arrow; Don Pablo, a little pudgy around the middle, always smiling and welcoming us into his home; and my favorite, Don Lelo, hunch-backed and probably not much more than five feet tall. Don

Lelo had to walk a long way from home to church, and he always had his cane in his right hand and his Bible in his left; his glasses kept sliding down his nose. What these three gentlemen had in common was their love for the Lord and their burden for family and others around them that they should also come to know Christ as their personal Savior.

Moving Into the Teen Years

Many of the teachers and other workers at Betania School were I-W fellas fulfilling their two years of alternative service and VSers who also came for a two-year service commitment. It was Mabel Miller, my seventh and eighth grade Home Economics teacher, who taught me to sew and got me started cooking. Kathryn Egli taught me cake decorating. Anna Rose was my seventh grade English teacher, who taught me how to diagram sentences. Ugh! Merle Sommers taught me to sing without sounding so breathy. Martha Kanagy was my piano teacher. I've honed all of these skills over the years and think of my teachers often. Gerald Wilson was the coach of the girls' softball team. I remember yelling at him one time when he took Ludi Díaz, the best pitcher ever, out of the game for some reason, and refused to bring her back in a later inning. How did I know that these were the rules of the game? Mr. Wilson never held this incident against me.

Early in my teens I began to teach Sunday School and Summer Bible School. Bible School was my favorite. I loved telling the Old Testament stories of baby Moses in the basket, Daniel in the lions' den, Joseph being sold into Egypt by his brothers, and David the shepherd boy, but I loved even more the story of Jesus' birth, life, death and resurrection. The kids would be glued to the ever-changing scenery of the flannelgraph board and the characters in the stories. And how they loved to sing the little choruses about Jesus!

Plenty of Pleasant Memories in Coamo Arriba

Early on, when we first moved to Pulguillas and lived on the "Hill," Daddy heard of a community called Coamo Arriba, and wondered if this might be a good place to start church services and Sunday School. The only way to get to Coamo Arriba was by horseback, about a 35-40 minute ride, up and down and around and around. The people he met on his first scouting trip were so happy and excited to have an evangelical pastor coming to preach and teach the Bible that it became a weekly Sunday afternoon occurrence. Daddy and Mother and sometimes Lydia or another person from Betania would saddle up their horses and head up and down the mountainside.

We kids got the horses ready for them on Saturday. We'd walk the four or five miles to the Ulrich Foundation in Asomante, round up the horses in the pasture, and ride them home. That was so much fun, and we thought we were pretty big stuff! Eventually they would build a chapel in Coamo Arriba, and what an ordeal it was. A cement mixer, cement blocks, bags of cement, 2x4s, rafters, huge pieces of corrugated metal roofing—everything was carried by muleback or horseback down this winding mountain trail.

As we grew into our teens, Coamo Arriba became a favorite place for all of us. We had great friends who lived there and we loved visiting in their homes. A couple of summers I got to spend two weeks there teaching Bible School. Yes, really...two weeks of Bible School! I don't know exactly when a road was built into Coamo Arriba, and even though we no longer had to ride a horse to get there, we had to have a four-wheel drive vehicle. Up and down we went, around and around, almost like the horse trail, and through a stream or two. One hill was so steep that I always was a little afraid that we might not make it.

In fact, one time Daddy, Jan, and one of our cousins that was visiting us had a really exciting experience on this very hill. The jeep had made it almost to the top when the engine suddenly died, and the brakes failed as well. As it began to roll backwards down the hill Daddy tried to steer it into the embankment on the left side of the road, but instead of just slowing down like he expected, it actually flipped over. Off the right side of this very narrow dirt road was a 2000 foot precipice, and the jeep came to rest right on the edge of it. It was somewhat of a teeter-tottery climb out of the vehicle! How many know that God will keep you safe when you've put your life in His hands and trust Him for direction and safety?

Christmas caroling was very special in Coamo Arriba. It was nearly an all-night affair! The young people—and some not quite so young—would hike up and down the hills, stopping to sing at almost every home in sight. No matter whether it was 9:00 p.m., midnight, or 3:00 a.m., the people would get up, invite us in, and offer us some amazing Christmas treats with coffee or lemonade. Those were the days, my friends!

Creating Alternative Enjoyment

I can't remember any times when being a Christian and a Mennonite necessarily made my life difficult. But when I was in high school, my very good friend, who with her brothers lived with their aunt, was saved. Her aunt was one of the most devout Catholic ladies I have ever known, and she was livid. My friend was not allowed to return home, and arrangements were made for her to live with two missionary ladies who offered her a place to live. Before long her aunt's heart softened, and my friend was allowed to return home. I'm confident that it was in large part because of her testimony that her aunt and her whole family came to Christ, and what a crusader for Christ she became! How many know that when you pray for God to move in someone's heart and life, and it looks like nothing is happening, you just keep right on praying. God will honor your prayers, I promise you.

As we grew into our teen years there were some things that Jan, Gene, and I weren't allowed to do. We couldn't go to the movies. We couldn't go to the *Fiestas Patronales*, which was a Catholic celebration of patron saints. It was sort of a carnival-type atmosphere with rides like at a fair, and it seemed like everybody else got to go and meet their friends at the plaza. Not us!

I also remember a big discussion about the high school prom when Jan was a senior. We were now attending the public high school in Aibonito. The dance was always held at the Bamboo Inn in Asomante, and an alternative celebration had to be offered so the Mennonite kids wouldn't want to go to the dance. Well, guess what? The party was at our house, and we really did have a fun night eating and telling stories and singing. The choice was clear—dancing at the Bamboo Inn or partying at the Hersheys' at Villa Alta!

Mennonite Gatherings

There were many occasions when all the Mennonite churches on the Island would get together for some kind of celebration. We always looked forward to Conference weekend in March. Usually it was held at Betania because it was the largest of all the church buildings. We didn't necessarily have to sit through the business meetings, which gave us the chance to hang out and catch up with our friends who we saw only once or twice a year. The other super cool get-together was Thanksgiving Day when we would once again meet at Betania Church. There would be a morning service, and afterwards a *lechón asado* (roast pig) lunch, complete with rice and beans. Then there would be a big auction as a fundraiser for Betania School. Daddy was often the auctioneer, and it was hilarious to hear him almost get his tongue all twisted up!

Many times the Mennonites worked closely with other denominations that were a little more established on the island, especially the Baptists and the Nazarenes in some of the larger cities. Daddy and his friend Alberto Espada Mata would preach at revival services in each other's churches. When Daddy was pastor at the church in Coamo, several denominations joined together for a special Easter service. The pastor from each church would preach on one or two of the last seven words (or phrases) of Jesus as He hung on the Cross. I have to admit that this could tend to get a little long and tedious sometimes, but it was all good.

The Mennonite church was all I knew as a child growing up in Puerto Rico. I was never "introduced" to it. Not only were my parents missionaries, but Daddy was also my pastor. We used to joke that every time the church doors were open the Hersheys would be there. Thursday night was always family night at our house, and one night after Daddy finished reading our bedtime story, I told him I wanted to accept Christ. I was six years old when he led me to Christ.

Over the years many missionaries from other places visited us, as well as people from the Mennonite Board of Missions and Charities. I was always fascinated by the adult conversations about the workings of the church in the different parts of the world.

Fond Memories of a Furlough

When I was in the third grade we came to the States on furlough and lived with Grandma Good in Illinois. It was a great year, as we met all of our aunts and uncles and cousins. We traveled to Niagara Falls on vacation and took the train to Pennsylvania to meet family on Daddy's side we children had never met.

The very best thing, however, that we did that year was the deputation tour. We drove from Illinois to Oregon for Mission Board meeting in a shiny green 1953 Chevy Bel-Air that a car dealer friend arranged for us to use while on furlough. We drove out and back by two different routes. During the day we enjoyed our time in places like Yosemite National Park, the Grand Canyon, and Petrified Forest, and at night we stopped for church...every night! Jan, Gene, and I would sing "Jesus Loves Me" in Spanish, I read the Scripture, Mother and Jan told stories about Puerto Rico in a children's meeting, and Daddy preached. All of this was for the purpose of raising support for the mission field. We left behind "prayer cards," a family photo card with our mission field address and a couple of Bible verse references about the Great Commission.

Years later, as a college freshman touring with the choir from Eastern Mennonite College at Easter break, I couldn't believe in how many church basements I saw my third grade photo tacked to the wall next to the Missionary World Map with a piece of yarn stretched from the photo to a little dot in the Caribbean called Puerto Rico. How funny!

Going Home Again

I love a good reunion, and it's so much fun to attend the Puerto Rico gatherings. There are former I-W guys and VSers from when I was two to 17, retired missionaries, MKs and PKs (preacher kids), former classmates from Betania who moved to the States to become college professors, pastors, housewives, and so much more. All these people had such a huge impact on my life. Some of them will never know.

Over the years I've been back to Puerto Rico many times. I have vacationed with family and friends, and I've even been there for just a day when my ship was in port. But my very best trip ever, bar none, was a couple years ago when my husband Cliff and I went back for the Academia Menonita Betania's 50th year school reunion. Cliff has a very vivid imagination, and although this was his first visit you would have thought that he was the one who grew in Puerto Rico instead of me! He loves telling stories, and sometimes they're almost unrecognizable, but he keeps right on telling them bigger and better! He fell in love with everyone he met, and can't wait to go back to see them. He loved every minute of playing tourist as we visited El Morro (my childhood hang-out!), Old San Juan, La Parguera, Ponce, Pulguillas, Aibonito, and La Plata. He understands much better now how my friends and my childhood experiences helped to shape me into the person that I am today.

I don't think I was prepared for the flood of emotions that overtook me when I returned to Betania after far too many years. Tears of joy mingled with those of my friends as we hugged and tried to catch up in such a short time. Seeing so many friends after 50 years brought back wonderful memories. I felt so welcomed by everyone, so loved; they were as happy to see me as I was to see them! When on Sunday morning Ana María, one of the ladies at Betania Church who probably was in her early 20s when I was a teenager, came up to the school to see me, I heard someone remark, "Man! Chela knows everybody!"

I've heard it said that you can't go home again. Not true.

Chapter 4

SUCEDIÓ EN MI BARRIO

Josian Rosario

Mi primer contacto con hermanos de la Iglesia Menonita fue a la edad de nueve años. Eso fue en el año 1948, cuando los hermanos T. K. Hershey, Lester Hershey y Paul Lauver llegaron al barrio Palo Hincado, donde nací y me crié.

Los Inicios de mi Congregación

Estos misioneros llegaron con el propósito de establecer una congregación. Tengo entendido que fueron comisionados a esta tarea por la Junta Menonita de Misiones y Cridades, cuya sede estaba en Elkhart, Indiana. Para esa fecha ya existían las congregaciones de Betania en Pulguillas, un barrio de Coamo muy próximo a Aibonito, y la de La Plata, en Aibonito. Eran congregaciones que se habían establecido hacía apenas dos o tres años.

El sitio donde iniciaron su trabajo en Palo Hincado fue justo detrás de la casa donde vivía mi familia. Las primeras actividades realizadas en el lugar despertaron el interés en algunas personas de la comunidad, entre las cuales me encontraba yo, un niño de nueve años.

Estos misioneros acostumbraban traer hermanos, especialmente jóvenes de La Plata y Pulguillas, en dos camiones, para estimular la asistencia de gente de la comunidad. Con el paso de un breve tiempo, un grupo de jóvenes, niños y adultos se interesaron en participar en las actividades y en apoyar el trabajo de los misioneros.

Después del trabajo de los primeros obreros, llegaron Wilbur y Grace Nachtigall a atender la misión. Con su labor la obra tomó un nuevo impulso. Desarrollaron un trabajo extraordinario y organizaron actividades que captaron el interés de todas las personas de diferentes edades, pero en especial el de los jóvenes.

Éste fue el tiempo en que fueron muy activos en la nueva congregación los hermanos Bernardino y Ramonita Miranda y su hijo Ángel Luis y demás miembros de la familia. También participaban activamente jóvenes y hermanos como Rubén Fuentes, Julio Rivera, Israel Hernández, Juan Hernández, Antonio Santiago, Lucía Santiago, Dolores Rivera, Mariana Rivera y Juanita Negrón. A todos éstos y a otros que mencionaré más adelante, tanto norteamericanos como puertorriqueños, les tengo un gran agradecimiento por contribuir extraordinariamente en mi formación. La influencia positiva de la comunidad cristiana que me rodeó fue clave en mi vida espiritual.

Los Campamentos de Verano

Durante la década del cincuenta, época de mi adolescencia, participé en eventos de la Iglesia Menonita en Puerto Rico que fijaron mi rumbo hacia el futuro. Una de las actividades fue los campamentos de verano. Tengo gratos recuerdos de estos campamentos celebrados en un lugar de Luquillo o Río Grande, propiedad de un Club de Rotarios. Era en un campo con una naturaleza majestuosa: un bosque, un río caudaloso, una piscina y un puente de hamaca.

Estos campamentos eran muy bien planificados de modo que no había desperdicio de tiempo. El personal que nos atendía era excelente. No recuerdo los nombres de todos, pero en su mayoría eran norteamericanos. Entre estos estaban Lawrence Greaser, Weldon Troyer, Lester Hershey y Elvin Snyder. Esteban Rivera y Melquiades Santiago eran algunos de los que preparaban los alimentos. Además, a cada participante se le asignaba un turno de trabajo, a menudo en la cocina u otra área.

El programa de estos campamentos era bien estructurado y se cumplía con puntualidad. La primera actividad del día era levantarse a las seis de la mañana a hacer ejercicios de calistenia en el parque de pelota. Le seguía el desayuno y las clases hasta el mediodía. Había clases de Biblia y manualidades. Después del almuerzo había tiempo para deportes y el uso de la piscina. Por la noche había una especie de culto devocional y entretenimiento. Al retirarnos a dormir celebrábamos en los dormitorios una lectura bíblica y un tiempo de oración. Las luces se apagaban a las diez de la noche

El costo de la matrícula era económico, pero aun así se ayudaba al participante para que pudiera asistir. En mi caso barría el templo y me pagaban $2.75 mensuales. Los ahorraba y pagaba mi matrícula.

Las manualidades eran sumamente educativas. Una de ellas fue hacer un porta biblias de madera. Tenía una cruz y las palabras Santa Biblia. Quizá algún participante conserve este trabajo. Otras manualidades eran las de trabajos en cuero.

Las Contribuciones de mis Pastores

Durante el pastorado del hermano Nachtigall en Palo Hincado hubo variadas actividades para jóvenes, intermedios y toda la congregación. No se limitaban a lo religioso. Se hacían actividades recreativas y deportivas. Recuerdo que aprendí a jugar juegos de mesa, tenis de mesa y volibol. Se participaba en deportes con los intermedios y los jóvenes de las congregaciones de La Plata y Betania. Por primera vez asistí a ver juegos profesionales de béisbol y de baloncesto en los parques Sixto Escobar en San Juan y el Paquito Montaner en Ponce. Ésas fueron experiencias inolvidables para jóvenes de un campo de Barranquitas. También se efectuaban giras al Viejo San Juan para conocer lugares de gran valor histórico, como El Morro.

El hermano John Driver fue nuestro segundo pastor. Éste me bautizó en el 1955 a los dieciséis años de edad. De este hermano tengo muy buenos recuerdos: su amor, paciencia, sabiduría, laboriosidad y entrega al Señor. Mantuvo un buen balance entre lo religioso y lo social.

Durante su pastorado se construyó el templo actual de la Iglesia Menonita en Palo Hincado. Recuerdo que en la etapa del empañetado me puso a empañetar en una pared. Yo no sabía hacerlo, pero él confiaba en la capacidad de aprendizaje de las personas, y eso me agradó. Al fin hice lo que pude, pero quedé complacido y alegre de haber podido hacer ese trabajo. Driver fue un buen ejemplo para mí y para muchos otros. Luego pastoreó la Iglesia Menonita de Summit Hills.

Otros hermanos con los que me relacioné fueron Don Heiser y su esposa Betty, quienes fueron pastores en Palo Hincado a finales de la década del cincuenta. Este hermano luchó mucho para que yo fuera clasificado como objetor por conciencia del servicio militar obligatorio cuando cumplí los dieciocho años. Don y Betty mostraron un amor y una dedicación a la obra entre nosotros que dejaron hondas huellas positivas en nuestras vidas. Su espíritu de servicio, humildad y sinceridad en su amistad eran notables. Dios bendiga a estos hermanos. No he sabido más de ellos desde su salida de Puerto Rico.

David Helmuth fue nuestro próximo pastor, a quien también admiré por su compromiso, amor y lealtad al Señor y su obra. Luego fue pastor en Summit Hills y director del Instituto Bíblico Menonita en Aibonito.

Otras Influencias

Aunque en mi niñez y adolescencia estuve bajo la influencia mayormente de misioneros menonitas norteamericanos, cabe mencionar que también hubo hermanas y hermanos puertorriqueños que ejercieron mucho bien en mi vida. Entre ellos quiero destacar al hermano José A. Santiago, pastor nuestro desde inicios de la década del sesenta. Conocí a Josian

Santiago como un líder destacado de la JEMP (Juventud Evangélica Menonita Puertorriqueña). En el 1960 vino a pastorear nuestra congregación. Ya yo iniciaba mi vida de adulto. Este amado hermano de espíritu misionero se había graduado del Instituto Bíblico Menonita en La Plata. Él y su esposa Agdelia realizaron un trabajo muy efectivo con los niños y los jóvenes.

Josian, además de ser mi pastor, fue mi gran amigo. Cuando vivía en Pennsylvania y venía a la Isla, siempre me visitaba. Mi primera experiencia de trabajo se la debo a él. Esto ocurrió en un periodo crítico de mi vida en el que yo acababa de recuperarme de una enfermedad. Toda su bondad, dedicación al trabajo, fidelidad al Señor, jovialidad y su fe me han sido de mucha bendición.

El hermano José M. Ortiz fue mi pastor a mediados de la década del sesenta. Para mí, este pastor joven era entusiasta, dado al estudio y comprometido con la obra de Dios. Aunque era de mi edad, no puse nunca en duda su capacidad por razón de su juventud. A él también incluyo entre los hermanos que me han ayudado en mi vida espiritual.

Contribución de las Damas en mi Formación Cristiana

Las hermanas menonitas, tanto esposas de mis pastores así como las misioneras, fueron vitales en mi formación cristiana. En nuestra congregación laboraron una hueste de hermanas muy dedicadas y fieles al Señor y a su obra. Entre otras, deseo mencionar a Grace Natchtigall, Bonnie Driver, Betty Heiser, Carol Glick, Ana Kay Massanari, Clara Springer, Ophia Snyder y Rosalina Ortiz.

Grace Nachtigall, esposa de Wilbur, era enfermera; una de las primeras en el Hospital Menonita en Puerto Rico. Fue un recurso bien valioso en Palo Hincado. Tenía un espíritu de servicio extraordinario. En muchas ocasiones atendió situaciones de emergencias de salud en la comunidad, tanto de día como de noche. A mi familia le prestó innumerables servicios relacionados con la salud. Uno de estos fue cuando mi madre tuvo su octavo alumbramiento en un Día de las Madres. Siempre me impactó su disposición desinteresada al servicio de los demás. Fue un brazo fuerte para su esposo en su trabajo pastoral. Era difícil no sentir agradecimiento hacia esta hermana.

Bonnie Driver, esposa de John, emanaba amor para todos. Poseía una paz y una dulzura admirables. Se ganó el aprecio de todos.

Carol Glick, trabajaba en la Academia Menonita Betania, pero vivía en Palo Hincado y asistía a nuestra congregación. Manejaba una camioneta repleta de estudiantes hasta la Academia. Era la maestra de los intermedios y los jóvenes en la iglesia y lo hacía con conocimiento bíblico y pedagógico. De ella aprendí a conocer el mejor manejo de la Biblia y mucho más.

Ana Kay Massanari, fue organista, maestra de escuela dominical y maestra en la Academia Menonita Betania. Tuvimos una bendición en contar con esta hermana en la congregación en Palo Hincado. Sin ella el trabajo con los niños hubiera sido muy cuesta arriba.

Clara Springer, esposa de Elmer Springer, hablaba mejor el español que él. Ellos atendieron la iglesia en un periodo de transición de un pastorado a otro. Apreciamos grandemente su trabajo durante ese tiempo en que nos alimentaron espiritualmente.

Ophia Snyder, esposa de Royal Snyder, lo ayudó mucho a atender nuestra iglesia durante un periodo corto, pero supo conquistar nuestros corazones. La bondad y el amor de estos hermanos eran inmensos.

A todas estas hermanas les ofrezco mi agradecimiento y mis bendiciones. Muchos aspectos de sus vidas han quedado impresos en mi corazón y en mi forma de ver a la mujer.

Conclusiones

Al realizar este corto escrito, tengo que reconocer que mi vida fue influenciada positivamente por la fraternidad y la amistad que pude establecer con todos los hermanos menonitas mencionados aquí, y los que no pude recordar. De hecho, de no haber podido conocer a esta apreciada gente, mi vida hubiera seguido otra ruta menos provechosa, pues el ambiente social que tenía en mi comunidad no era el mejor. También agradezco a mis padres que nunca me impidieron la relación con los menonitas, sino que, por el contrario, siempre la estimularon. La confraternización de estos hermanos con mi familia ha resultado en que muchos de los descendientes están afiliados a diferentes iglesias evangélicas, o practican valores aprendidos a través de la Iglesia Menonita.

Chapter 5

HOW PARASITES CHANGED MY LIFE

Juan A. Rolón

Before I begin my story of becoming a Mennonite, I will tell you something that means so much to me.

In the 1940s my family didn't know the Americans who lived in La Plata, but we saw them driving by our house almost every day. Our house was located close to the road between La Plata and Aibonito. Eventually they started stopping by to say "Hello" and to check on the welfare of our family. My parents, Juan Rolón and Aurora Cartagena de Rolón, had seven children; I'm the oldest. These American Mennonites realized that we were all full of parasites, and wanted to help us. They started bringing us medicine for the parasites. To this day I still remember having to drink a glass of bitter liquid, followed by swallowing two giant-sized pills. The treatment was effective and appreciated, but it was definitely not pleasant. Now knowing that many children died due to having parasites, I am so grateful that the Mennonites were concerned enough to care for us medically.

Joining the Mennonite Community

The Mennonites also cared for the spiritual welfare of my family and me. We would see them driving by our house regularly, and we always would wave and call out, *"Adiós, americanos."* Sometimes they stopped to visit and to give us Bible tracts.

In the summer of 1957 two people, Armando Rolón and Royal Snyder, came to our home to invite us children to the La Plata Summer Bible School. My parents gave permission for us to attend even though our family was Roman Catholic. They also invited our family to attend services at the church in La Plata. My father and we children accepted the invitation and began attending regularly. My mother joined us about six months later.

After going to church in La Plata for about one year, we began attending services in Aibonito, where a new congregation was being started. Services were held in the Audición Luz y Verdad building. Two other families also chose to attend services in Aibonito. Eventually a church building, Iglesia Evangélica Menonita, was built, and is still being used. One by one my family became Christians and joined the Mennonite church.

Going to a Mennonite School

During the same summer that we joined the church, my parents were asked and gave permission for us children to attend Escuela Menonita Betania, the denominational school located in Pulguillas. I had been unable to pass the eighth grade at the public school because I failed English and mathematics. At Betania, though, I was in a small class of ten students consisting of two boys and eight girls. There I received excellent teaching, and eventually graduated from ninth grade. My classmates were awesome and we had lots of fun together. Those two years attending Betania were the best ones in my school experience. The teachers were great, and my North American teachers were very influential in my process of learning English.

Roberto Camacho, also a student, became a good friend then, and our friendship still continues today. I remember spending the night once with Roberto. His family raised thousands of chickens. That night I helped them gather chickens to sell to a processing and butchering plant called To-Ricos, in nearby Asomante.

High School and Other Significant Experiences

When we graduated from Betania, and went on to the public high school in Aibonito, we kept pretty much to ourselves, and didn't participate in some activities such as attending dances and the prom. We would meet every Wednesday for Bible study at the Ehret Funeral Home, which was located across from our school. Also we had our own banquet and graduation party.

During my high school years I was more interested in sports than studying. I was very involved in intramurals of baseball, softball, basketball, volleyball, track and field, and ping pong. These sports were played against other grades rather than against other schools.

I enjoyed our church's youth activities. Our *Jóvenes* (Mennonite Youth Fellowship) group had activities such as Bible study, playing games, performing dramas for the church congregation, going to the beach, and attending a yearly camp which included young people from other Puerto Rican Mennonite churches. The week-long camp was a lot of fun and we learned more about the Bible and Jesus as well as learning new games and making new friends. It was a good experience to spend some time as president of the youth group, too.

I chose not to go to college, and instead worked part-time for Hospital General Menonita. My job was washing the hospital vehicles and that was where I learned to drive. Our pastor, Lawrence "Lorenzo" Greaser, drove me to Guayama to get my driver's license when I was nineteen years old. After that I was able to pick up people and take them to church on Sunday mornings and Wednesday evenings.

It was at that time that I had an unfortunate experience. I was walking to the Mennonite hospital with my friend Pepito Fernández to meet some friends from the Voluntary Service unit, and was hit by a car. Lorenzo lived about two houses from the accident, so Pepito went to get him and they took me to the hospital. I was hospitalized for one month with two fractures in my pelvis and a fractured knee. I never found out who hit me and was very angry for a long time. Through praying and the prayers of my family and church friends, I was finally able to forgive the driver of the hit-and-run car. I had to spend a long time doing physical therapy, and was unable to work for about one year after the accident.

Becoming a Conscientious Objector

I had barely recovered from the accident when I received my draft notice. This occurred during the Vietnam War. Lorenzo explained the option of becoming a conscientious objector rather than being part of the United States military. After much thought and prayer, I decided to become a conscientious objector.

Lorenzo soon found a place to serve a two-year I-W term, Ryder Memorial Hospital, in Humacao. Fortunately for us, the hospital accepted both my friend Pepito and me. There it was suggested that it would be good for us to take the two-year licensed practical nursing course. We agreed, and this decision has given me many opportunities during my life.

Close to the end of my term I asked for, and was granted, a transfer to the Hospital General Menonita in Aibonito. There I had the opportunity to live in the Voluntary Service house with a large group of volunteers. One of the members, Odette Leininger, from Archbold, Ohio was serving as a registered nurse. She and I began dating, and later got married on October 1967. We moved to Ohio where for many years we have been members of West Clinton Mennonite Church, near Pettisville.

For me, that simple invitation in the 1950s from those Mennonite workers of La Plata changed my life completely. Through their caring and concern for me and my family, I became a Christian. In addition, fortunately, I got rid of those undesireable parasites!

Chapter 6

ENCRUCIJADAS INESPERADAS

Rafael Falcón

Las encrucijadas de mi niñez llegaban a mi vida de forma inesperada y hasta inadvertida. Atento a la familia y los amigos, a la escuela y la iglesia, y con todo un mundo por explorar, mi vida tomó giros importantes que supe apreciar sólo con el tiempo. Estas encrucijadas aparecían repentinamente, y me ofrecían de forma generosa una dirección distinta que me llevaba camino a unas amistades más amplias, percepciones más profundas y nuevas oportunidades. Atribuyo mi falta de reflexión sobre el cauce que tomaba mi vida al hecho de que a esa edad las grandes decisiones que me afectaban no las tomaba yo, sino los adultos de mi entorno. Por cierto, fueron mis padres los que hicieron el primer cambio direccional significativo para que yo me criara menonita en Puerto Rico.

Mis Padres

Mi padre Ramón Falcón Vázquez era el hijo menor de Mónico y Eustaquia, y vivía en el sector la Curva de la Guitarra del pueblo de Comerío. Monche, como lo conocían, tuvo que dedicarse a ayudar en la finquita de sus padres, y por esa razón abandonó la escuela al finalizar el segundo grado. Su madre murió inesperadamente cuando Monche tenía apenas trece años. Por eso Rafael, su hermano mayor, lo crió y por consiguiente todo el mundo pensaba que Monche era su hijo.

Rafael, el hermano de mi papá, había llegado a tener éxito económico en el mundo de las vacas y las fincas, y había mudado a su familia a Aibonito en las primeras décadas del siglo veinte. Allí prosperó mucho más en el negocio de la piedra, la arena y el bloque de cemento, y fundó lo que se conoció como Canteras Falcón. Fue en este hogar y en este fresco pueblito de la montaña donde creció mi papá. Allí, también, crió a nuestra familia, manteniéndonos a través de los años con carros públicos, tiendas de ropa, restaurantes y la crianza de pollos.

Mi papá vio por primera vez a mi mamá, una linda jíbarita, montada en un hermoso caballo blanco, y le resplandecieron sus grandes ojos azules. Ana, mi futura mamá, vio a mi papá y le encantaron esos mismos ojos azules. Él se le acercó porque el caballo no obedecía la orden de caminar ni los ruegos de la joven desesperada. Estaba "emperrao", como decía mi abuelo Marcos Meléndez cuando sucedía esto con su caballo.

Monche, que sabía algo de caballos, hizo la magia para que el equino echara a caminar. De esta manera echó a caminar también una relación con Ana Luisa Meléndez. Este romance terminó en matrimonio en 1945 y la crianza de seis hijos. Entre esta media docena de críos estaba yo, Ángel Rafael Falcón Meléndez, el mayor.

Con Metodistas y Católicos

Mis padres eran de tradición católica. Sin embargo, me matricularon en un jardín de la infancia de la Iglesia Metodista que quedaba en una esquina frente a la plaza del pueblo. Para mi familia la asistencia a esta escuela era más conveniente, y, además, no había muchas otras posibilidades en el pueblito.

A decir verdad, no tengo muchas memorias de esa etapa de mi vida. Poseo una imagen borrosa de que nos ponían a tomar siestas en unas mantas en la parte de arriba de la iglesia. Algo que sí recuerdo vivamente es que tenía una maestra trigueñita que era bien buena gente. Su presencia continuó conmigo por muchos años. Cuando me veía en el pueblo, ya hecho un hombrecito, me saludaba afablemente y me llamaba por mi nombre. Este amable gesto me hacía sentir muy bien.

Para el primero y el segundo grados me matricularon en el Colegio Católico Sagrado Corazón, ubicado en la salida de Aibonito hacia el pueblo sureño de Salinas. El Colegio quedaba precisamente un poco más arriba de la casa del patriota puertorriqueño Federico Degetau y González, y un poco más arriba también de la casa en donde yo había nacido unos seis años antes. Aquí, mis maestras eran monjitas católicas que llevaban unos hábitos blancos que me llamaban mucho la atención. El director era un sacerdote español bajito con una sotana negra grande, una pronunciación diferente a la que yo estaba acostumbrado, y unos espejuelos de marco de carey con lentes como fondo de botella.

Mis compañeros pertenecían a las familias más adineradas e influyentes del pueblo. Algunos eran hijos de los estadounidenses que venían de administradores de la fábrica de guantes que tenía oficinas centrales en los Estados Unidos. Otros eran los hijos de los comerciantes, los hacendados y los profesionales del pueblo.

Cuando asistía a la Iglesia Católica para actividades del Colegio siempre me quedaba fascinado por todas las estatuas de santos. También me impresionaba lo imponente del histórico edificio, construido durante la soberanía española en la segunda mitad del siglo diecinueve.

En una ocasión participé en un dramita navideño donde hice el papel de Melchor y llevaba una vestimenta reluciente, una corona llena de "joyas" y un cofrecito con oro. Ya terminado el dramita, mis padres me tomaron una foto en blanco y negro con "Gaspar" y "Baltazar" en el atrio de la iglesia. Ese momento fue bien especial. Mis padres habían tomado prestada la cámara que mi primo Cástulo había comprado en Alemania cuando estuvo en el ejército—y no se la prestaba a nadie.

Aventuras en la Finquita

En ese tiempo nos mudamos de una casa en el pueblo que quedaba cerca de la casa alcaldía a una finquita de tres cuerdas en el barrio Robles, entre Aibonito y el barrio La Plata. La sangre campesina de mi padre lo había llamado, y él respondió sin vacilación. Para mí fue una tremenda bendición que papi siguió su instinto jíbaro, pues ahí pasé algunos de los mejores años de mi vida.

La finquita estaba en una "jalda" y tenía una casa grande de dos pisos con un majestuoso balcón y un espacioso garaje. El garaje era uno de los pocos del barrio, pues no había mucha gente en ese tiempo que tenía carro. Mi padre era uno de los afortunados de no tener que caminar, coger un carro público o viajar por guagua para llegar al pueblo. Por eso siempre lo ocupaban cuando había una emergencia en el barrio. "Don Monche, lléveme al hospital porque Margarita se paró en una botella rota y se cortó el talón". "Compay Monche, lléveme a emergencias porque Cristóbal se hirió la mano con un machete bien 'afilao'". Éstas eran algunas de las peticiones de los vecinos que mi padre satisfacía con mucho gusto. "Don Monche es un hombre servicial", yo escuché decir a los del barrio en innumerables ocasiones.

Durante nuestros años en la finquita hubo una elección política que nunca olvidaré. Los carros subían de La Plata con escobas frente a las llantas delanteras. Jamás había visto esto. Mi padre me dijo que era para evitar que los clavos y las tachuelas que pusieron los partidos opositores poncharan las llantas e impidiera que llegaran los votantes.

También en estos meses de elecciones pasaban vehículos con enormes altoparlantes en la capota tocando una pegajosa canción con ritmo de marcha militar que decía: "Jalda arriba va cantando el popular, jalda arriba siempre alegre va riendo…". Los carros llevaban también unas banderas blancas con letras rojas que leían Partido Popular Democrático y tenían la silueta de un jíbaro con un sombrero de paja y las palabras "pan, tierra, libertad".

Mi padre me explicó que ése era el partido del entonces gobernador don Luis Muñoz Marín. Me dijo también que Muñoz Marín era el primer gobernador elegido por el pueblo puertorriqueño, y que los anteriores habían sido nombrados por el gobierno de los Estados Unidos. Señaló, entonces, que su partido apoyaba el estado libre asociado para la Isla. Yo entendía un poquito mejor lo de la independencia o lo de la estadidad, pero lo del estadolibrismo, no tanto.

En la finquita comencé a tenerle amor y respeto a la tierra y a los animales. Teníamos pollos, cerdos, gallinas, cabras, perros y un caballo. Cuando dije respeto a los animales, no estoy mintiendo. Siempre pensaba que yo era más fuerte que cualquier cabro. Punto. Pero Facundo, el cabrote blanco con la mancha negra en la cabeza, me demostró lo contrario.

Un día me dio la descabellada idea de agarrar la soga de Facundo y enroscármela por el cuello. Mi intención era simplemente comprobar que podría controlar y detener un cabro con sólo el cuello. Repito: con sólo el cuello…sin las manos o los brazos.

Facundo, sin embargo, tenía su propio plan: seguir sus fuertes instintos cabríos. Así que, repentinamente me encontré en un viaje meteórico. Me arrastró por toda la finquita, cuesta abajo y cuesta arriba. La soga, tensa y áspera, hacía su penoso recorrido por mi cuello. Después de algunos angustiosos minutos, que me parecieron años, la soga finalizó su recorrido. Facundo, dejándome todo maltrecho, continuó campante entre las matas de plátano, como diciendo: "Rafaelito, ¿quién es más fuerte?". Yo, por mi parte, me quedé allí boca abajo con el cuello ensangrentado y bien adolorido. Todavía peor, me quedé con el honor marchitado.

Del amor y del respeto a la tierra podría narrarles varias experiencias. Aprendí con mi papá que cuando las matas de guineo tienen muchos hijos, éstos se trasplantan a otro lugar para que prosperen, crezcan y produzcan. Aprendí que da gusto localizar las batatas ocultas en la tierra con un "perrillo", una especie de machete delgado y afilado. Aprendí también que aunque las guayabas del vecino estén más maduras y jugosas que las de tu finquita, uno no debe cruzar la verja en su búsqueda. ¿Sabes por qué? Porque el mayordomo te puede perseguir, te puedes caer y cortarte la rodilla, y les pueden notificar la fechoría a tus padres.

El Encuentro con los Menonitas

En ese tiempo en mi barrio no vivían muchas personas. La mayoría era gente humilde y sin pretensiones que respondía a los apellidos comunes de Torres, Rosario, Collazo, Rolón y Ortiz. Una de las familias bien conocidas era la de don Abraham y doña Carmen Ortiz, que tenían un taller de mecánica a unos cien metros de nuestra casa en dirección al pueblo.

Mi padre era uno de esos católicos nominales que en ocasiones, a petición del sacerdote de la parroquia, dirigía las actividades religiosas del barrio, pero no asistía a la iglesia ni vivía una vida cristiana ejemplar. Sin embargo, papi tenía inquietudes espirituales y estaba en la búsqueda de un cambio. Nuestra vecina, doña Carmen, le había hablado en varias ocasiones de unos menonitas que tenían una iglesia en La Plata, donde ella asistía. Un día ella lo invitó a los servicios, mi padre aceptó la invitación, y deseaba llevar a la familia también.

Mi madre no saltó de entusiasmo ante la idea de asistir a una iglesia menonita. Ella se había criado bien católica, sus padres asistían a la iglesia con regularidad y su papá hasta cantaba rosarios en las actividades de la Iglesia Católica. Además, los menonitas eran prácticamente desconocidos en la Isla, pues hacía apenas unos doce años que habían llegado, y se habían establecido en sectores rurales de la zona montañosa isleña. Ella sabía de los metodistas, los bautistas y los presbiterianos, pero no mucho de los menonitas. Sólo sabía que tenían un hospital muy bueno en La Plata y una escuelita en Pulguillas. También pensaba—pero no estaba bien segura—que el dentista que le había hecho el último trabajo era menonita.

Después de muchas conversaciones, mi familia acordó asistir a un servicio dominical en la Iglesia Menonita de La Plata.

Esa mañana de 1955 la pequeña iglesia estaba repleta de nacionales y estadounidenses. El edificio de concreto, con sus dos atractivas palmas reales en el frente, era pequeño y sencillo. En su interior tenía unos doce o catorce bancos, un púlpito y una cruz sin un Cristo crucificado en la pared detrás del púlpito. En la parte trasera había un tablero con números en blanco y negro que indicaban la asistencia del día, la del domingo anterior y la cantidad recaudada en la ofrenda.

El pastor, con un leve acento estadounidense, dirigió con energía y convicción, y nos dio una cordial bienvenida. Luego se cantaron dos himnos de un libro azul que yo nunca había visto. Dos señores, uno alto y rubio y el otro bajito y trigueñito, recogieron lo que llamaron "ofrenda". El pastor predicó, y mi padre se sintió bien contento porque el mensaje era en español y no en latín. Al salir del "servicio", como ellos lo llamaron, el pastor nos dio la mano a todos. Yo me sentí pertenecer. También nos dijo que regresáramos, y así lo hicimos.

Uno de los domingos, el pastor, que vivía al lado de la iglesia en una casa verde de concreto, nos invitó a almorzar en su casa. Para mí la experiencia fue única e inolvidable, pues comimos alimentos a los que no estábamos acostumbrados. Nos sirvieron pollo horneado, papas majadas, una salsita blanca y espesa para las papas, habichuelas tiernas y pan casero con jalea.

También nos dieron postre. Esto fue muy especial, pues nosotros casi nunca terminábamos las comidas con algo dulce. Cuando se daba la ocasión, siempre era dulce de lechosa con queso, casquito de guayaba con queso, los añorados plátanos en almíbar que hacía mi papá, o algo así. Pero este postre me llamó mucho la atención: era una materia verde traslúcida que temblaba muchísimo al pasarse. Miré a mi hermana Anabel. Ella meneó la cabeza como diciéndome: "no tengo la mínima idea". Entonces, me atreví a preguntar tímidamente a la esposa del pastor. "Gelatina", me contestó con toda naturalidad. Se llamara como se llamara, esa desconocida "tambaleante materia" estaba sabrosa, y me la comí con mucho gusto.

Durante el almuerzo me di cuenta que se pasaban los platos para que nos sirviéramos lo que deseábamos comer. Noté también que se prefería que dejáramos el plato completamente limpio. En mi casa, por el otro lado, mami nos daba todo listo en un plato, y nosotros sabíamos que no teníamos que comernos todo. Si dejábamos el plato limpio, mami pensaba que todavía teníamos hambre, y nos servía otra porción.

Una Escuela Menonita Incrustada en las Montañas

Continuamos asistiendo a la iglesia y mis padres se bautizaron en la Iglesia Menonita de La Plata. Varios meses después se hizo la decisión de matricularme en la Escuela Menonita Betania. La escuela, que había sido fundada por misioneros en las postrimerías de la década de 1940, quedaba a unas seis o siete millas de mi casa. Un camión Chevrolet azul llegó a recogerme muy temprano.

El camión había sido adaptado para transportar estudiantes. La adaptación consistía en poner cuatro bancos de madera en la parte trasera, un techo, y una escalera de tubos de plomería. Los asientos eran de una madera áspera y sumamente dura, sin ningún tipo de cojín para apaciguar los golpes de los muchos hoyos que agarraba el camión en su travesía. El techo era de la madera más barata que se habría podido conseguir en aquella época, pero nos protegía del viento, de la lluvia y del picante sol caribeño.

De todas las adaptaciones, la escalera de tubos era la más notable, y la más famosa entre el estudiantado. Había que deslizarla para que pudiéramos subirnos y bajarnos del vehículo. Si uno tenía las manos en el tubo en que ocurría el deslizamiento, la malvada daba unos pinchazos que te dejaban chillando y maldiciendo al creador de ese monstruo. La marca te quedaba por semanas como muestra de haber sido una víctima más de la empedernida escalera. A pesar de las marcas y de los pinchazos, tuve que admirar la ingenuidad de esos menonitas estadounidenses.

El camión, que había salido de La Plata, pasó por Aibonito para seguir recogiendo estudiantes. Se dirigió entonces hacia el pueblo de Coamo, pero en el barrio Asomante volteó hacia la derecha en busca de otro barrio llamado Pulguillas. La carretera subía y bajaba en un zigzagueo continuo, y aunque la distancia a recorrer no era considerable, las muchas paradas y las decenas de curvas hacían que el viaje pareciera una eternidad. Finalmente pasamos un puentecito que por su estilo parecía haber sido construido durante el tiempo de la dominación española. Inmediatamente, frente a un cafetal, comenzamos a subir un empinado camino de tierra de unos cien metros.

Llegamos a un lugar donde había tres casas de concreto, una pintada de amarillo y dos de blanco. También había dos casitas blancas de madera. En el pequeño estacionamiento vi varios carros y otro camión Chevrolet de color verde. Este vehículo tenía la misma adaptación que la del azul, y, por supuesto, el mismo tipo de escalera. Luego supe que ese camión verde se usaba para transportar a los estudiantes que venían de Palo Hincado, un barrio de Barranquitas en donde los menonitas tenían una iglesia.

Cuando miré del estacionamiento hacia la loma vi unos edificios de concreto grandes pintados de blanco y verde. Luego supe que éstos eran los salones de clase para los intermedios. Un maestro rubio y alto, que cargaba un maletín de cuero, me informó amigablemente que el salón de tercer grado quedaba en el último de los edificios del lado derecho.

Después de una corta orientación de la directora, nuestra maestra nos guio a los del tercer grado al salón de clases. En nuestra caminata hacia el salon, noté unos gigantescos columpios y unos frondosos árboles de guamá que nunca imaginé iban a ser testigos mudos, por muchos años, de mis aventuras betanienses.

Patricia Brenneman, nuestra maestra, se presentó y nos impartió instrucciones. La Srta. Brenneman sabía español muy bien porque había vivido en Argentina, donde sus padres habían sido misioneros menonitas. Luego supe que ella había vivido en este país suramericano por unos siete años, y que había acabado de llegar a Puerto Rico como misionera. Así que los dos éramos novatos en Betania.

De Nombres, Apellidos y Sobrenombres

Algo que me llamó la atención en Betania fue que no sólo la maestra era estadounidense, pero también un buen número de los alumnos. Escuché nombres y apellidos que me costaba pronunciarlos y a los que mis oídos no estaban acostumbrados: Hershey, Greaser, Lehman, Snyder, Springer, Nauman, Birky y Holderread, entre otros. Nosotros queríamos adaptar los nombres y los apellidos a nuestro español, y decíamos, por ejemplo, Esnyder, Espringer, Birqui, Jerchi y Jólderi.

Algunas veces estos nombres anglosajones hasta se cambiaban para adaptarlos a nuestras necesidades. Había una maestra estadounidense a la que llamaban señorita Playa. Siempre creí que su apellido era muy interesante y diferente para una menonita de los Estados Unidos. Tal vez llevaba este apellido porque tenía sangre italiana o portuguesa. Años después me di cuenta que su apellido verdadero era Beachy, uno muy común entre los menonitas angloparlantes. Quizás la administración de Betania había hecho la adaptación para asegurarse que los estudiantes no lo confundieran con "bicho". Posiblemente, la razón del cambio era que este vocablo, que en el mundo hispanohablante en general simplemente significa insecto, en suelo boricua adquiere un significado sexual vulgar. Estoy seguro que el ingenioso cambio le evitó muchas burlas, sonrisitas y momentos vergonzosos a "la señorita Playa".

Otro incidente relacionado con nombres fue el de mi amigo y compañero de clases Eugene Hershey. A Eugene, el hijo menor del conocido misionero menonita Lester T. Hershey, todo el mundo lo conocía como Yuyín. Para mí era un apodo interesante porque nunca lo había oído, ni tampoco conocía a alguien a quien llamaran así. En innumerables ocasiones había escuchado Quique, Cuco, Pepe, Paco y Vitín, pero Yuyín, nunca. Años después me di cuenta que el apodo era una adaptación fonética de su nombre. Estos cambios le facilitaban el asunto de la pronunciación al puertorriqueño que "masticaba" principalmente el español, y que todavía en esa época no estaba bien familiarizado con nombres que procedían de raíz angloparlante.

Entre los directores de mis años en Betania llegó un estadounidense que en su primer año administrativo prohibió absolutamente el uso de apodos en la escuela. A su parecer esa práctica y esa tradición eran ofensivas y de muy mal gusto. Todo el que violara esta "ley" tenía que vérselas con el director y sufrir las consecuencias. La tarea fue ardua porque en la sociedad boricua era muy difícil refrenarse de usar apodos. Para mí era como decirles a los estudiantes isleños que no podían comer arroz y habichuelas.

Algunas Personas Singulares

En mis años en Betania hubo una considerable cantidad de personas que me impresionaron y tuvieron un gran impacto en mi vida. Doña Venancia Martínez, una de las cocineras que trabajó en la escuela por muchísimos años, es una que siempre recordaré. Ella vio a cientos de estudiantes pasar con su bandeja metálica para que les sirviera los acostumbrados arroz, habichuelas, vegetales, postre y leche en polvo. A mí me alimentó en todas mis etapas betanienses: estudiante, maestro y director. Su honestidad, humildad, responsabilidad y amabilidad eran sorprendentes. Una sonrisa irradiaba por su cara siempre que la veía, y me demostraba que estaba orgullosa de mí. Ella sabía que me había alimentado físicamente en Betania. Sin embargo, más importante para mí es que lo había hecho igualmente en forma espiritual.

Otra persona importante en mi vida fue Carol Glick, la directora de Betania por muchísimos años, y una de las figuras emblemáticas de la institución. La admiré porque en esa época era una de las pocas mujeres en la Isla que tenía licencia para manejar camiones, pero esta admiración era más amplia. La valoré por ser una mujer emprendedora, humanitaria y extremadamente comprometida con su fe cristiana. También, la respeté porque creyó en mí y en mis habilidades. Recibí su apoyo incondicional y firme cuando fui estudiante, y después cuando fui maestro novato durante su liderato administrativo. Sin embargo, sentí este respaldo más claramente cuando hizo posible que yo, a la joven edad de veinticinco años, fuera su sucesor en la dirección de la escuela que ella respetaba y amaba con todo su corazón.

Viajes a la Fundación Ulrich

Algo que hice rutinariamente durante mis primeros años en Betania fue viajar a la Fundación Ulrich después del día escolar para jugar con compañeros de clase y amigos. Algunas veces caminaba. En otras ocasiones iba en una destartalada bicicleta que de vez en cuando me dejaba a pie.

El recorrido me llevaba cuesta arriba y cuesta abajo. En la subida tenía que pasar por la acentuada curva de Mr. Brown. Nunca comprendí el porqué del nombre cuando los que vivían en una preciosa casa en esa curva eran los Rolón. Entonces, en la bajada pasaba por unas casas que reflejaban opulencia y riqueza.

Aproximándome a mi destino pasaba por dos edificios que me llamaban mucho la atención. Uno era una ermita blanca con una cruz en el techo y cuatro columnas al estilo romano. En ocasiones me detenía para admirar la estructura y, aunque el portón de rejas con candado me impedía acercarme, pude leer una inscripción en la parte superior: "Capilla de Nuestra Señora de los Desamparados". En otra línea se podía ver que la ermita estaba dedicada a la memoria de una señora de apellido Serrallés.

El otro edificio que despertaba mi curiosidad era una casilla de camineros. A través de la historia ahí había vivido el encargado de mantener un sector de la carretera que iba de Aibonito a Cayey. En estos años de mi niñez la larga estructura de piedra y ladrillo albergaba a varios de mis compañeros de juego.

Ya en los terrenos de la Fundación, después de pasar por un gigantesco portón, uno inmediatamente notaba al lado izquierdo una enorme casa blanca. La majestuosa estructura, construida a principios del siglo veinte, se conocía en el pueblo como Villa Julita. Las instalaciones habían sido la casa de veraneo de la famosa familia Serrallés—los del conocido Ron Don Q. En los años de mi niñez la casa llevaba el nombre de Aibonito Hall, y servía de residencia del personal de la Fundación Ulrich. Ahí vivían varios de mis camaradas de aventuras que llevaban los apellidos de Greaser y Springer.

Los terrenos de la Fundación Ulrich proveían un rico campo de juego para nosotros. Sin duda alguna, los partidos de béisbol, con una pelota medio deshilada y un bate agrietado, dominaban las actividades. Pero había mucho más. Nosotros invadíamos el taller de mecánica para admirar los logros de los hábiles empleados con los carros y la maquinaria de la Fundación. Visitábamos la tiendita de los terrenos para comprarnos un mantecado, una paleta, un bombón o un refresco por seis chavos para apaciguar la sed. Jugábamos de escondido en los alrededores del polvorín, el cual se había usado para almacenar explosivos durante la construcción de la Carretera Central en el siglo diecinueve. A veces merodeábamos por las siembras de legumbres y frutas. Siempre recuerdo la primera vez que probé las sabrosas y jugosas "fresas americanas", como se llamaban para distinguirlas de las fresas nativas que se daban dondequiera.

Una Escuela Pública en el Pueblo

Me gradué de noveno grado de Betania en 1962 con otros diez compañeros. La mayoría de los graduandos era del grupo original de tercer grado, y el resto eran otros que se nos habían unido en el trayecto. Nunca voy a olvidar a esos compañeros que me ofrecieron su incondicional amistad, la cual cultivo hasta hoy día.

Siempre pensé asistir a la Academia Bautista de Barranquitas como habían hecho otros amigos menonitas después que se graduaron de Betania. Esto no se logró. La Academia Bautista cerró sus puertas el mismo año que me gradué de Betania. Así que tuve que matricularme en la escuela superior pública de Aibonito que llevaba el nombre de Bonifacio Sánchez Jiménez. No estaba muy entusiasmado con la decisión, pero la única otra posibilidad era regresar al Colegio Católico.

A tres de los estudiantes que llegamos de Betania nos colocaron en el 10-1, el grupo más avanzado de los seis de décimo grado. Yo sabía que los cambios iban a ser significativos para mí. Estaba cambiando de una educación privada religiosa a una pública secular, y de unos grupos pequeños a unos grandísimos.

Los que llegamos de Betania fuimos fichados de "diferentes". No bailábamos, no tomábamos alcohol, no fumábamos y no íbamos al cine, entre otras diferencias. Estos valores atesorados en Betania se convertirían ahora en la causa de las bromas, las insinuaciones y los abusos verbales. "¿Que tú eres meno...qué?", nos decían cuando tratábamos de explicarles que éramos menonitas, o "Tú eres meno...na", cuando tratábamos de defender nuestras acciones.

Sin embargo, estos atributos que no eran valorados por muchos, eran admirados por otros, tanto profesores como estudiantes. Muchas veces escuchamos decir de profesores que podían confiar en nosotros, y hasta dejarnos solos durante un examen porque éramos menonitas. También los estudiantes se referían a nosotros como personas decentes con valores nobles.

Nunca participé en los famosos bailes ni en las tremendas fiestas que se celebraban muy a menudo durante mis tres años de estudio. Sin embargo, quería asistir a por lo menos el baile de graduación de cuarto año. Hice el esfuerzo de aprender a bailar y tomé "lecciones" con varios compañeros que sabían "menear el esqueleto" mejor que yo. Además, me compré un traje azul marino, una corbata a la moda y unos zapatos de la tienda La Aiboniteña. Hasta mi amigo Cuco tomó tiempo para enseñarme a hacerle el nudo a la corbata.

Desafortunadamente, estos emprendedores gestos no impresionaron mucho a mi padre. No aprobó que yo asistiera. Sencillamente, no permitió que yo participara en esa "actividad mundanal". Él desaprobaba rotundamente la idea de que yo fuera acompañado por mi amiga especial, la que llevaba mi sortija de graduación, y yo la de ella. Pero más fuerte que todo, a mi parecer, era que ella era católica. Siempre recuerdo a los otros compañeros dialogando varios días después de lo mucho que gozaron en el baile de graduación y yo, mientras tanto, me mordía los labios.

Dinamismo en la Iglesia Menonita de Aibonito

Cuando nos mudamos del barrio Robles a Aibonito comenzamos a asistir a la Iglesia Menonita del pueblo. Allí pasé mis mejores años de actividades inolvidables en la vida de la iglesia: el coro, las escuelas bíblicas de verano, los dramas navideños y de Semana Santa, los campamentos de verano, las sociedades de jóvenes y de intermedios, las cantatas de ocasiones especiales, y muchas más.

En esta etapa aprendí a ser más compasivo y a desarrollar liderato gracias a las experiencias que se me presentaron y a las personas que hicieron esto posible. En nuestra congregación se celebraban elecciones anuales para los diferentes puestos con la intención de promover así participación y liderazgo. Un año me seleccionaron como uno de los candidatos para servir de ujier, y un compañero de clases y yo tuvimos el honor de ganar la votación. Así que íbamos a ser ujieres. Los dos anticipábamos entusiasmados la ocasión de servirle por primera vez a la iglesia en forma oficial.

El siguiente domingo llegamos bien temprano listos para recibir a la gente y repartir los boletines. Para nuestra sorpresa y confusión vimos a un señor, que había sido ujier por muchos años, con los boletines en la mano esperando a la gente. Mi amigo y yo nos miramos. Cómo le íbamos a decir a este respetado hermano que nosotros habíamos ganado la elección y se suponía que lo reemplazáramos. Decidimos que yo fuera a informarle la situación al pastor Lawrence Greaser. Su reacción, a lo que consideré ser una delicada y difícil situación, me tomó por sorpresa. "¿Qué piensas de tener cuatro ujieres en lugar de dos? De esta manera no lo ofendemos", me dijo calmadamente. Aunque al principio lo tomé como un escape a la confrontación, después me di cuenta que era una actitud sabia y llena de compasión. Así que ese año terminamos siendo cuatro ujieres en lugar de dos, y comenzó de esta forma una nueva tradición en la Iglesia Menonita de Aibonito.

De esta época recuerdo a los pastores Lawrence Greaser, John Driver, Samuel Rolón, Ambrosio Encarnación y Don Heiser. Fue durante el pastorado de Driver que yo estaba en la edad del posible reclutamiento militar. Quería declararme objetor por conciencia, pero no sabía cómo manifestar esta postura, y aún menos llenar un formulario que era totalmente en inglés. Driver vino al rescate, me orientó y me ayudó a llenar los papeles. Un tiempo después recibí la clasificación deseada de acuerdo a mi posición pacifista.

También en esos momentos de mi vida buscaba una universidad para continuar mis estudios. Driver me recomendó Hesston College, y hasta me ayudó a llenar la solicitud que era en inglés. Sin embargo, después de todo este esfuerzo decidí asistir a la Universidad Interamericana de Puerto Rico en San Germán. Tomé esta importante decisión, en gran parte, porque mi padre pensaba que la universidad menonita estadounidense era "ridículamente cara", y que el estado de Kansas "quedaba muy lejos de mi casa".

A Más de Medio Siglo del Encuentro

Todo en la vida tiene sus consecuencias y sus resultados. No hay la menor duda que el hecho de haberme criado menonita en Puerto Rico ha impactado enormemente mi vida en un sinnúmero de formas. Estoy seguro que hoy día no contaría con la comunidad fraternal con la que comparto. Esto lo confirma, por ejemplo, que muchos de los amigos que tengo en las redes sociales son de la conexión menonita en Puerto Rico, establecida hace ya más de medio siglo. También lo comprueba el grupo de amigos con el enlace menonita-boricua que nos reunimos en Goshen, Indiana, una vez al mes. Claro está, que muchas de las conversaciones que disfrutamos se centran en historias relacionadas con el haberse criado menonita en Puerto Rico.

En innumerables ocasiones me he preguntado cómo hubiera sido mi vida si mi padre no hubiera aceptado la invitación de la vecina a asistir a esa pequeña iglesia menonita en el valle de La Plata. De esto no podría proveerles una contestación clara y precisa. Lo que sí puedo afirmar con certeza, en este momento de mi vida, es que en nuestro trayecto por la vida siempre tenemos que pasar por encrucijadas inesperadas.

Chapter 7

THE BEST GIFT MY PARENTS GAVE ME

Carolyn Holderread Heggen

While I did not spend my entire childhood in Puerto Rico, the years there made an indelible impression and were profoundly significant in my subsequent life. I believe the best gift my parents gave me was the opportunity to spend those formative years in another culture, learning Spanish and expanding my worldview beyond that which would have been mine as a child born into a small, ethnically homogeneous, rural Idaho community.

In the early 1940s my mother, Rachel Schiffler, and my father, Wilbur Holderread, made their way separately to the rural community of Castañer, Puerto Rico, where the Church of the Brethren operated a small hospital. My mother, a recent graduate of the La Junta Mennonite School of Nursing in Colorado, was sent by the Mennonite Board of Missions and Charities to Castañer to be director of nurses.

My father, a conscientious objector during World War II, was assigned to work as an ambulance driver and handyman at the same hospital. Mom said he won her heart with the tasty strawberries and tender lettuce he grew in the hospital garden and personally delivered to her doorstep. In 1944 they were married in a pasture next to the hospital with Wilbur and Grace Nachtigall, Mennonite volunteers in La Plata, serving as their attendants. Most of the Castañer community turned out for the post-wedding celebration at which the nursing staff presided in fancy aprons my mother made.

I was born two years later, just three weeks after my very pregnant and seasickness-plagued mother traveled alone from San Juan to Galveston, Texas, on a freight ship, the only way she was able to join Wilbur, who had been transferred by his draft board, before her due date.

For the first nine years of my life our family lived in Idaho where my mother worked as a nurse and my father taught in high schools. My parents often talked about their experiences and friends in Puerto Rico and would sometimes speak to each other in Spanish, particularly when they had secrets to share. How excited we all were when my father was recruited by the Ulrich Foundation, a Mennonite organization that supplemented the activities of the Mennonite Board of Mission and Charities, to be the manager of their experimental dairy farm in Asomante, Puerto Rico!

A New Home

After a long train ride, my first, from Idaho to New York, we boarded an Eastern Airlines plane for Puerto Rico. It was 1956, years before there were smoking restrictions on airplanes. My excitement at flying for the first time, and in going to the island of which my parents had spoken so often and so fondly, was tempered by the splitting headache and asthma symptoms I experienced from spending hours on an airplane with too many smokers. My physical discomfort was forgotten when someone shouted, "There it is!" and I too spotted the beautiful green island in the brilliant blue waters below. As the plane dropped lower and lower, I feared we would miss the runway and end up in the ocean.

Having left the United States in winter, it was a pleasant jolt to step off the plane into warm tropical breezes. It was a relief when Lawrence Greaser, director of the Ulrich Foundation's work on the Island, spotted us, the only debarking obviously

North American family of five, and waved to identify himself as the one who would drive us to our new home in Asomante.

We arrived late at night and after parental assignment of beds, quickly fell asleep. How exciting it was to awaken the next morning and see the stunning views from our south-facing house: a lush valley with gentle hills, the towns of Coamo and Ponce, and most thrilling for those transplants from landlocked Idaho, the Caribbean Sea and Caja de Muertos Island.

While marveling at the spectacular view, we heard children's voices coming from a small house on the hill facing ours. "Come to me! Come to me!" they yelled in broken English. We guessed it was an invitation to come and play, which we later would do when we learned enough Spanish and figured out how to circumvent the rugged valley between our homes.

My New School

But for now our top priorities were to unpack, settle into our house, and get enrolled at Academia Menonita Betania. What an exciting but frightening thing it was when our parents, having completed the enrollment process, left us with principal Carol Glick who took my sister, Cathy, to Srta. Mercedes Meléndez's second grade room, and me to the combined third and fourth grade class. Our brother David, just three, was not yet old enough to enroll in school.

Patricia Brenneman (later to marry Fidel Santiago) was my teacher. I was relieved to see I had a teacher who could speak English, but was chagrined to learn she thought I would learn Spanish more quickly if, after the first few days, she would only speak Spanish. Perhaps she was right because by the end of the first semester I could say most of what any 10-year-old wants or needs to say. Decades later, as a 40-year-old, I would try to learn Urdu in Pakistan and then again, as a 55-year-old, I studied Nepali. These later forays across linguistic boundaries highlighted how fortunate I was to have been exposed to Spanish when my brain was more agile.

It is surprising how much I remember from that first semester these 60 years later. I recall my sadness and surprise that one of my classmates didn't have shoes to wear to school. I was impressed with the thick callouses on his feet and how he could run over sticks and stones without wincing. I remember how skilled some of my classmates were with tops (*trompos*) and how the girls played jacks with small stones. I had never experienced tropical rainstorms and remember how happy I was with the frequent afternoon rains that crashed against the tin roofs of our classroom with such force that it was impossible to hear Srta. Brenneman's voice, and we could read till the rains stopped. I remember the pain of knowing my classmates were talking about me and laughing but not knowing what they were saying. I remember how one of my classmates would sometimes pinch me and make me cry. I finally realized she was jealous because the girl she had considered her best friend had started playing with me at recess. After that I tried to make sure we included her in our activities.

I remember how difficult it was to swallow the big blobs of thick peanut butter given by the US Department of Agriculture and occasionally served in the school cafeteria. While I loved the taste, the consistency made it hard to swallow without bread. My mother reminded me of how much harder to eat the peanut butter would be for Puerto Ricans who were not accustomed to the taste. While I loved the cold milk we drank at home, I found it hard to enjoy the warm powdered milk served at school. There was no refrigeration in the school kitchen. Some North American children brought cans of Nestlé Instant Cocoa mix to add to their milk, making it more palatable. When I lobbied for cocoa, mother said that unless all the children were able to have it, I most certainly could not bring cocoa to school. How I loved the rice and beans served most days, particularly when Doña Venancia brought me a piece of *pegao*, the crispy rice that had stuck to the bottom of the cooking pan. Years later when I returned to Betania as a teacher, Doña Venancia again gave me the crunchy delight.

The next year Carlos Lugo was the fifth and sixth grade teacher. Some of the boys took new interest in their appearance. Many now carried a comb in their pocket, and after recess headed straight for the mirror on the wall where they would carefully part their hair and pat it into place. Many of us girls wore braids or pony tails and could not so easily repair our messed-up hair. The boy's vanity was surely related to their developing interest in girls and the notes they sometimes sent asking us to "be my girlfriend."

I remember Mr. Lugo's frequent reference to the country of Nepal. I now wonder why he was so intrigued by this Asian country so far from the Caribbean and one he had not visited. He referred to it as *"el techo del mundo."* As a child who loved to climb trees, I was intrigued by that image and held the fantasy that Nepal was so high that if you were there you could look down on all the world. Years later when my husband Richard and I worked there for Mennonite Central Committee, I took advantage of every chance I had to trek into the high Himalayan Mountains and often thought of Mr. Lugo's description. While I never climbed high enough to look down on the whole world, I certainly saw spectacular scenery.

Purgantes and an Unexpected Confinement

My mother was anxious to resume nursing. Several days a week she helped one of the Mennonite doctors from Aibonito hold a community medical clinic on the school grounds in the small *casita* that would be my English classroom years later when I returned as a teacher. One of her duties was to check students for lice and send home the treatment powder for those infected. This sometimes included her own daughters.

Another duty was to periodically give all Betania students *purgantes* to purge them of intestinal parasites. The government-issued medicine must have been unusually strong one time because many of us vomited and felt weak and crampy afterwards. She spread blankets under large trees behind the cafeteria and those of us who were most affected spent the rest of the day in this makeshift "hospital." Some of the students, surely in jest, wondered aloud if my mother had tried to kill them. I remember being glad that I too had a difficult reaction as it would surely absolve my mother of malicious intent. Most often I was glad when my mother was on campus because she took great care in bandaging wounds and treating injuries and was a respected, beloved person on campus.

One of my most poignant memories of Betania was the morning when all students from third to ninth grade were summoned to the upper campus for a mass gathering. A visibly upset and agitated Miss Glick reported that a bad word had been found written on the wall of the bathroom, and that we would be kept in the assembly room until someone admitted to having written the unidentified word. No recess, no lunch, no bathroom break until someone confessed!

I spent the morning of confinement trying to imagine a word so bad that it merited this severe a response. The only word bad enough that I could think of was "Devil" or possibly "Hell." When someone finally confessed (and his identity is not what I remember about this story) and we were released, I asked the Snyder twins, Edith and Esther, if they knew what the offending word was. They did, and told me. It was a Spanish word I'd never heard before so they told me the crude English equivalent, also unknown to me. They rolled their eyes in disbelief at my naiveté and ignorance.

Life on the Foundation Farm

How different my life was from what it had been in Idaho. Most of the time I was grateful to be living in Puerto Rico. I loved the freedom to run around on the large Foundation farm chasing butterflies, hunting guavas, exploring cow paths, pretending I was an intrepid explorer discovering new lands. There were a number of horses that belonged to the farm and others that boarded there, including the horse Lester Hershey used on Sunday afternoons to ride to Coamo Arriba where he led worship services. Sometimes I was allowed to ride one, and as for many young girls on horses, there was a thrilling sense of power and freedom.

We felt safe on the farm and knew we could count on one of the many workers to help us if we got lost or hurt. Don Pepe Rosado was the highly respected farm majordomo, and my father depended on him for many things. He was trustworthy, dependable, and ingenious. His one weakness, my father noted, was that even though he did learn to drive a tractor, he was never able to master the art of going in reverse. My father was quite sure this was because he'd not had a tricycle as a child.

My father loved the Spanish language and had learned to speak it quite well when he'd lived in Castañer as a younger man. Back on the Island, he was determined to learn two new words a day and carried a small notebook in his pocket in which he wrote the new words he wanted to remember and incorporate into his speech. Don Pepe Rosado spoke elegant Spanish and was often the source of Dad's new words or idioms.

In Idaho my father had been a high school teacher of industrial arts and agriculture. When our family moved back to the United States, he pursued a graduate degree in Modern Languages, later teaching Spanish for the rest of his working days, a career change he was happy to have made.

On the farm there was both an upright and an underground silo. My siblings and I loved tasting the molasses that was mixed with the chopped grass. We also enjoyed watching the workers fill the silos and later retrieve the silage. One day while looking over the edge of a silo to watch the workers below, I leaned in too far and fell, hitting my head on the corner of the metal box with pulleys used to bring up the feed and workmen. The resultant gash on my skull bled profusely and I passed out. Don Pepe brought me to the surface in the feed box and ran, carrying me, to our house. We were both covered with blood by the time he made it to the top of the hill. I appeared more seriously hurt than I was. My frightened mother stopped the bleeding, revived me, and found my father who drove us to the

Mennonite Hospital where Dr. Ben Kenagy sewed me up. I still have a raised scar on my scalp, a reminder of the price one sometimes pays for exuberant curiosity.

The Ill-Tempered Guinea Hen

That is not my only bloody memory from the years on the farm. My mother's midwife fee for pre-natal, delivery, and post-natal care was $10 or "whatever." On several memorable occasions parents who already had many children and few financial resources wanted her to adopt their newborn child as payment. Sister Cathy and I wished she would accept their generous offer, but Mom explained that caring for a real baby was not like playing with dolls and reminded us we were all too busy with other responsibilities to take on one more. She mollified us by saying that when we returned to the States perhaps we could acquire another sibling. How delighted we were when eight months after our return to Idaho sister Marilyn was born!

Payment for Mom's midwife services usually came from the "whatever" category and the most frequent payment was a stalk of bananas. We ate lots of fresh bananas during those years and mother developed an impressive repertoire of recipes featuring the fruit: banana pancakes, banana cupcakes, banana cookies, banana ice cream, banana pudding, and the family favorite—frozen bananas on a stick.

The most memorable payment she received was a large and ill-tempered guinea hen. A bit of background is in order. My father and two farm workers had dealt with a strange-acting cow. I remember him saying "She thinks she's a reindeer!" as we watched her leap over fences. The cow was a valuable pure-bred Holstein from Minnesota that had been part of a herd shipped to Puerto Rico to reproduce and improve the milk production capabilities of native dairy cows. My mother, always the nurse, suspected the cow had rabies, a realistic concern given the number of rabid mongooses known to live in the hills of central Puerto Rico.

After calling the Department of Agriculture, my father followed their directives and with the help of two workers, caught the suspect bovine, killed her, and cut off her head, which they put on dry ice and transported to the Department of Health in San Juan. When tests indicated that yes, the cow indeed had rabies, the three men who had been exposed to her foaming saliva were immediately hospitalized in San Juan and for 14 days received a daily rabies shot. These treatments were brutal, and I remember my father saying he wondered if it wouldn't be better to die than suffer the preventative measures.

While Dad was hospitalized in San Juan, back in Asomante we tried to keep the guinea hen contained. Whatever enclosure we devised, the foul fowl pulled a Houdini-worthy escape. He pecked whoever tried to catch him and squawked day and night. At one point my usually gentle mother said, "I'd like to make soup out of that bird!" We children were delighted with the suggestion. She confessed she had never killed an animal and was quite sure she couldn't start now. Dad, the family butcher, was hospitalized and would be incapacitated for some time after returning home. I was only a fourth grader, but felt confident that for the sake of a little peace and quiet I could dispatch the offensive critter.

My mother, delighted with my offer, sharpened the household machete. She helped me find a log, and told me what to do. Then she put on protective gloves, caught the guinea hen, handed him to me, and pulled my little sister and brother out of sight of what was about to transpire. Heart pounding, I took a deep breath, placed the hen's head on the chopping block, raised the machete high above my head, and brought it downward in a grand and energetic whack. Unfortunately, about halfway down I panicked and tried to stop. But my arm already had such momentum that I was unable to stop and the machete continued downward with diminished force. Instead of severing the head of the poor bird, I only partially cut his neck while simultaneously letting go of machete and bird, and letting out a blood-curdling scream.

My mother, quite sure I had cut my foot instead of the hen's head, came running out of the house. By now the hen was spouting blood from his neck wound and was thrashing up against our white house while emitting horrifying sounds. My mother, crying and yelling "You have to finish him off—he's suffering!" grabbed him and gave him back to me. Haunted by what I had done and crying in horror and fear, I hysterically whacked and whacked the bird to a definitive death, leaving his carcass so mutilated that he wasn't fit even for the soup pot. We quickly buried him instead. I have never intentionally killed another animal since then, and am quite confident I will never again try.

Santa Clara Storms In

Another memorable experience occurred in August of 1956. In the middle of the night I awoke to the sound of strange voices in our house. I jumped out of bed to investigate, and discovered that dozens of people from the neighborhood had left their wooden houses and come to wait out a forecasted hurricane in our sturdier cement block home. For the first time hurricane warnings had been broadcast on television, and word of the impending Santa Clara hurricane spread across the Island. People were urged to find safe shelters.

As a child unaware of the dangers of hurricanes, it was exciting to awaken to a houseful of friends and neighbors. The men helped Dad board up our large glass windows, and the women helped Mom prepare a simple breakfast. We children brought out our toys and set up one of the bedrooms as a playroom.

Once the storm began, the sounds of the raging winds and of objects being slammed against the house were frightening. Had we not been with many of our neighbors it surely would have been even more terrifying. Mom played hymns on the piano to try and mask the disturbing sounds outside. After several hours of dramatic wind and rain, the eye of the storm passed over us and the men stepped out to inspect the damage.

The total stillness of this stage was haunting after the preceding pandemonium.

My siblings and I were heartbroken when Dad reported that our chicken hutch with 12 hens in wire cages had disappeared. We guessed their corpses had landed in Coamo, or perhaps even in Ponce. The men scurried around the area looking for animals or people who might be hurt, but were careful to get back inside before the calm of the eye passed and the violent winds began once more.

The ferocious winds of 120 mph did extensive damage to property and to crops. Santa Clara was the most destructive hurricane to hit the island in almost 25 years. Over 1,000 homes in Aibonito alone were destroyed and many more damaged. Because a significant number of trees had been uprooted and had fallen across roads, it was many days before we were able to get into town. Miraculously, only 16 lives were lost, but many of the coffee plantations would never recover. One of the happy surprises was to discover that while the first half of the storm had indeed carried away our chicken pen, the second half had blown it back up the valley and slammed it against our house, not far from its original location. That one of the chickens was still alive and had laid an egg was something I long considered to be the first real miracle I'd witnessed.

Moving into a Religious Identity

I suppose there were a few Catholics in Buhl, Idaho, but I didn't know any. What a change it was to move to a predominately Catholic community. I was intrigued by the elegance of the Aibonito Catholic church and loved the mesmerizing cadence of the "*Santa María, madre de Dios…*" rosary prayer that Catholic friends would mumble with minimal provocation. But the ubiquitous pictures of Jesus with his heart outside his body and bloody crucifixion images were confusing and disturbing. Even more upsetting were some of the stories Mennonite friends told me, the most haunting being the report, surely fictional, of nuns impregnated by priests being forced to throw their newborns into a well behind the local church.

A common belief in Puerto Rican Mennonite circles was that Catholics worshiped a dead God, or worse, that they worshiped Mary. It was made clear that one was either a Christian or a Catholic. Imagine my surprise on a recent trip to Aibonito to see La Casa Ulrich being used by a group of Protestant ministers (including Mennonites) and Catholic priests to gather in prayer for the healing of their city!

But my childhood years were minimally influenced by ecumenical forces. Christian faith, practice, and communal identity as understood by Anabaptist Mennonites had been important to my family in Idaho and continued after moving to Puerto Rico. We quickly learned where and when Mennonites gathered for worship, and chose the Pulguillas congregation as ours.

My father was employed by the Mennonite-connected Ulrich Foundation and my mother volunteered at medical clinics run by staff from the Mennonite Hospital in Aibonito. Betania was staffed by mostly Mennonite volunteers and paid employees, and thus had a distinctive Mennonite Christian flavor. We had devotions and prayer each morning in the classrooms and prayed before lunch each day. Occasionally we would have chapel services in the Pulguillas church building and Lester Hershey and other pastors led devotions and Bible studies.

One chapel service that impacted me greatly was led by a visiting missionary of a different denomination who shared an evangelistic message. Was his name Mr. Scott, or was he perhaps a Scottish missionary? I don't remember those details, but I do remember clearly his flannelgraph presentation. He shared the story of Jesus, the good shepherd, and told how Jesus loves us each so much that he'd go looking for us if we were lost. He then presented a gripping message with the use of cut-out hearts of different colors. He said we are a lost sheep if we haven't invited Jesus into our heart. He put a big black heart on the flannel board to demonstrate what our "unsaved" heart looks like. He then placed a red heart to represent the blood of Jesus and a lily-white heart to show what our hearts can look like if we accept Jesus.

I'd seen photos in my mother's nursing textbooks of the blackened, deformed lungs of long-time smokers. I certainly didn't want a heart that looked like those and quickly raised my hand when offered the chance to invite Jesus into my "black" heart. I now wonder if darker-skinned students were offended by this object lesson. And I wonder if I had any sense of the racist connotations of this questionable evangelistic tool.

Lester Hershey was given the names of those children who had raised our hands and he met alone with each of us, prayed for us, and talked about getting ready for baptism. He explained that as Christians we should read the Bible every day and pray, so I began trying to read the Bible in a methodical way for the first time. I began with Genesis although my mother suggested I might want to start with the New Testament. I was a diligent student and never started reading other books halfway through, so was determined to start at the beginning and work my way through to the end. My admirable determination faltered somewhere in the middle of the book of Joshua where I found the stories much too violent and frightening. I wondered if boys and men found the stories more tolerable, and wished there were more stories about girls and women that might appeal to me.

On the day before my baptism, my mother gave me $10 and told me I could go by myself to Aibonito on a *público* to buy a special dress for my baptism at the department store. The combination of going into town by myself, being given money to buy a dress on my own, and being baptized—all on the same weekend—felt like a huge leap forward in growing up.

In my spiritual immaturity I found that the most significant change after my baptism was that now I got to wear a pretty mantilla to church. Fortunately my baptism as a child of 12 was just the first step on a long journey, trying to understand what it means to develop an authentic faith that empowers one to better live as a faithful follower of Jesus. I'm still wondering and learning.

Significant Connections through the Community of Faith

When I was in seventh grade our family was asked to help with the worship services at the Mennonite Church in Coamo. I enjoyed the people and active youth group, but my, how I dreaded the curvy drive and the resultant car sickness. My father taught adult Sunday school, my mother and I taught the children's class, and I played the piano. How I dreaded hearing the chorister announce the hymn *"Un Día"*—it had way too many flats (five) and accidentals for my skill level. Because the congregation sang hymns with a Latino rhythm with much more joy and energy than those that had been merely translated from North American English hymns into Spanish (some of which themselves had been translated originally from German into English), I wished we'd always sing Latino-composed songs. This difference was still apparent in recent worship experiences in Puerto Rico.

The Coamo congregation was blessed with a core group of energetic, creative, hardworking young people. They wrote original dramas at Christmas and Easter, crafted the props and costumes, and then performed the dramas in Coamo and around the island in other churches. This talented group included Enrique Ortiz and his sister Aida, Cristino Rodríquez, his sister María de los Ángeles and his cousin, Edgardo Cordero.

On Wednesday nights at the Pulguillas Church there was Bible study and prayer meetings for adults and activities for children and young people. Most of the participants were students at Betania and were my friends. What fun we had together doing crafts and learning new songs. Until our most recent move I still had the hanging flower vase made from a cow's horn that I, along with the other participants in these fun

Wednesday night meetings, sanded and varnished into something of which we were very proud.

Sometimes after the Wednesday night activities, my parents would stay and we would listen in as some of the VSers made radio contact with a group of missionary aviators who were serving in Ecuador. I remember how concerned the radio operators in Pulguillas were one night when they could not make contact as arranged. It was later learned they had been massacred by the Huaorani (also known as Auca) Indians. When books were later written and movies made about this tragedy, I felt a personal connection to the story.

Another Puerto Rico experience that connected me to a significant historical event was spending a day with Nathan Leopold who in 1924, along with Richard Loeb, committed what they hoped would be the "perfect crime." I had not heard of this crime nor the murderers, but when the Ulrich Foundation families were invited to the annual Play Day at the hospital grounds in Castañer, my parents told us we would meet a very interesting person—a man who had once been a murderer, had spent 34 years in jail, and was now trying to do something good with his life. We were both excited and frightened.

Once in Castañer, it was surprising to see that Nathan looked just like the Mennonite and Church of the Brethren workers, although he often left the group to smoke. As an adult I have read several books about Leopold's crime, and have marveled that in the hills of rural Puerto Rico I had spent a day playing volleyball and picnicking with a group that included this infamous killer. And when I later studied and taught restorative justice principles, I thought with gratitude of the Church of the Brethren's willingness to let him live and work with them as he attempted to make symbolic amends and do reparations.

The Importance of Those Years on the Island

It is of course impossible to know how different my life would be were it not for those formative years in Puerto Rico. Fluency in Spanish has opened professional doors and allowed me to develop meaningful, deep relationships with Spanish-speaking people in the United States and throughout Latin America. My world view was enlarged, and I developed a sense of global citizenship that would have been unlikely had I not left rural Idaho. Having lived in Puerto Rico and later in Pakistan and Nepal makes me impatient with those who cling to a view of US exceptionalism.

There were things that were difficult: being away from extended family and not being able to see my beloved grandmother before she died, feeling like an excluded outsider before I learned enough Spanish to talk to my classmates and participate in their games, being the brunt of jokes I didn't understand, and having to assume too much responsibility for the care of my younger siblings when mother was off delivering babies. But the delights and benefits far outweighed the losses and difficulties. I will always be grateful for the gift of those years and the lasting values and relationships formed.

Chapter 8

SICK COWS, JOY RIDES, AND OTHER PUERTO RICAN ADVENTURES

Ted Springer

In August, 1968, I left Puerto Rico on my way to college in Hesston, Kansas. As the plane left the airstrip from San Juan International Airport and flew toward the eastern tip of the Island, I was reminded of the many trips we had taken to the beach on a private seaside farm in Fajardo to which we had been granted access for many years. This had come about by a business relationship that Bob Ehret, a Mennonite family friend of ours, had developed years before with a local businessman in Fajardo whose family owned the property. We would simply show a letter of passage to the gatekeeper, who lived at the entrance with his family, and we would be allowed to enter into, what to me, was the most beautiful pristine beach I could imagine. Protected by outlying coral reefs, the shoreline was usually calm even if the Atlantic Ocean was rough. Probably due to its isolation, the grass flats of this beach were a haven for all forms of seashells and thousands of starfish. A bit further out were beautiful reefs brimming with hard and soft corals, sponges, anemones, and countless species of colorful fish. This is where I developed my love of the sea and the marine life contained in it.

As our airplane made the banking turn and headed back west toward the United States mainland, I could see the Island's shoreline where angry Atlantic waves crashed into the rocks in the Dorado-Vega Baja area. Here also I had spent childhood days enjoying the beach in the sheltered pools protected by massive rock formations. Now, my eyes followed the patchwork of forested and grassy slopes rising from the coastal areas up into the central mountains which had been my home. I watched the western tip of the Island disappear, and realized this marked the end of life as I had known it for my first 18 years. I had to wonder when I would return to the island I called home, along with all the familiar places and people I loved.

The Way It Started

My parents, Elmer and Clara Springer, along with my brother Fred, had boarded a freighter to Puerto Rico in 1947, having responded to a call they felt to serve on the Island under the Mennonite Board of Missions and Charities. They had left their farm implement dealership in Fisher, Illinois, at the urging of Dr. George Troyer who, during a short visit back to the States, was getting his car refueled at the dealership, which also served as a gas station. He had told them of the work being done by the Mennonites to address the many needs on the Island. So my folks joined the project in Pulguillas, where a new church had been established and medical care was provided through a clinic. Elmer was involved with project administration and the many ongoing church, home, and school construction projects. Clara was busy with church activities and serving the educational needs of the rural children.

At first, the Spanish language was a challenge for all three family members, so they relied heavily on missionaries Paul and Lois Lauver who had preceded them to Puerto Rico, were fluent in Spanish, and had established the church in Pulguillas. Beulah Litwiller also joined the project work to help with education. Having grown up in a missionary family in Argentina, she was fluent in Spanish as well.

In the summer of 1948, Clara and Beulah combed the hillsides in the Pulguillas area, visiting the homes of families who were attending the young church, to enlist children for the school. That August they started the Academia Menonita Betania under the auspices of the Mennonite Board of Missions and Charities.

My brother Fred attended the Baptist Academy in Barranquitas along with Weldon Troyer, son of George and Katherine Troyer. They would board at the Academy during the week and then return by public transportation to Pulguillas on the weekends.

My First Years

It was into this setting I was born in January of 1950 in La Plata. Here, the Mennonite work in Puerto Rico had begun in 1943, and the first hospital was established in a converted tobacco warehouse. My brother Fred, 17 years my senior, left for college in the States when I was six months old. I obviously have no recollection of these early years, but have seen home movies of me rolling my first birthday cake down the hill in the yard next to our home, while Lester Hershey's children, all older than I, helped recover it.

Soon other churches were planted in surrounding areas in the interior of the Island, and the church and school in Pulguillas were well established. More North American volunteers, I-W workers, and individuals from local communities were joining the work. So when Wilbur and Grace Nachtigall left for the United States on furlough, my parents were asked to provide leadership for the new Mennonite church in Palo Hincado. Neither of my parents were preachers, so they handled the administrative duties, served as chorister, Sunday school teachers, and were the missionary presence in the community. They relied on Ángel Luis Miranda and other gifted members from the congregation to do the preaching.

At some point during our time in Palo Hincado a home was built, into which we moved. As the construction neared completion, a 55-gallon drum of water was being used to soak tiles prior to setting them into the floor. One day I climbed onto a block that was set against the side of the drum and bent over to peer at the mosquito larvae wiggling in the water. Of course, the block slid aside and I tumbled head first into the drum. Before Mother could arrive to save me, I had found a way to turn myself around and pop my head out while holding on to the sides of the drum. I must have been quite a sight because, once my mother figured out I was unharmed, she couldn't help but laugh at me.

Ulrich Foundation Action Up Close

A few years later my parents were asked to move to the big house known as "Aibonito Hall" on the outskirts of Aibonito. They were to be houseparents for the I-W men and other volunteers serving under the Ulrich Foundation, Inc., a private non-profit corporation started and completely funded by Raymond and Verda Ulrich from Roanoke, Illinois. This foundation, while closely aligned with the Mennonite Board of Missions and Charities, had ongoing projects in the areas of soil conservation, poultry husbandry, vegetable production, dairy husbandry, artificial insemination of dairy cattle, and pasture improvement. It also established a much-needed dental health program. These services not only helped improve the immediate needs in the communities, but had the primary goal of educating and enabling people to develop opportunities to help themselves.

Many people were needed to carry out these programs and many were housed in Aibonito Hall. This is where my first real memories of life in Puerto Rico begin. I can remember sitting at breakfast with all the men and women volunteers as the boxes of cereal were passed around the table. Conversation was always lively. There was true camaraderie and a sense of accomplishment from work worth doing. Seeing all this activity at a young age, I was instilled with the belief that nearly anything was possible if one set their mind to it.

Everywhere one turned there were new structures being built, new things brought to life where only scrub grass had existed before. To this day I can remember the smell of the earth as a bulldozer cut a new road or leveled off a foundation for a new building. Local and State-side personnel were working together to bring about positive change, whether it was on the farm in Aibonito, the farm in Asomante, the school in Pulguillas, various new church sites, the dental clinics established in the area, or the new Mennonite Hospital built on donated land on the edge of the Ulrich Foundation farm.

Never Alone

We didn't have relatives nearby, although several of my aunts served as volunteers in Puerto Rico at various times. I grew up as an only child since my brother was gone to college before I got to know him. However, we were never at a loss for "family." Life for me centered around church work, the Betania school, general mission work, and Ulrich Foundation projects. I lived in 13 different homes during my 18 years in Puerto Rico, but was always surrounded by many of the same families and classmates, so that I didn't identify home as a specific house, but rather a community of caring people.

My parents hosted many visitors from the United States over the years. It seemed nearly every Sunday someone came for dinner. It was fun to sit at the table and listen to the variety of stories and experiences shared on those occasions. I remember one such meal which was rather embarrassing for my mother. After prayer, the food was passed and everyone was involved in lively conversation. My mother would get up occasionally to get something in the kitchen. It wasn't until she went to get the fresh pie she had baked the day before, however, that she realized she had forgotten to serve the pot roast still in the oven. Everyone got a hearty laugh out of it at her expense.

First-time visitors to the Island were always awed by the panoramic vistas as we traveled the winding roads of the Cordillera Central. From various vantage points one might see all the way to the Atlantic Ocean to the north. Shortly thereafter, one might see the city of Ponce and the Caribbean

Sea to the south. On some foggy mornings, the mountain peaks would tower above the blanket of fog which had settled in the valleys below, a beautiful sight in the morning sunlight. A favorite view of mine was following the line of flamboyant trees, with their multitude of flowers in a variety of red and orange hues, planted along the roads which zig-zagged up and down the mountain sides.

On Bovine and Kid Adventures

Like most young boys I was quite active, and living in a sub-tropical climate year round meant I spent a lot of time outdoors. However, I was prone to get into trouble from time to time. My first recollection of such a time was early in life during our first stint of living in Aibonito Hall. One evening shortly after dark I decided to disrupt the evening for a couple of the I-W men by standing outside their bedroom window and making a loud ruckus. As soon as they got up to see what was going on, I ran out of sight. Once they went back to their business, I crept back and started making noise again, and then ran out of sight. I guess I was too young to realize they were on to me by the third time I returned. The fact, that this time the lights were off in their room, should have been a clue. Well, when I started my noisemaking I was greeted by a pailfull of water, launched my way through the window screen, which completely drenched me and dampened my fun. Luckily, they must not have told my parents, and I never mentioned it to anyone. Lesson learned.

Living on the 160-acre farm purchased by the Ulrich Foundation provided many diverse experiences and opportunities for exploration. Not only was Aibonito Hall located on this property, but it was also the farm where the poultry and the fruit and vegetable projects were started. There was also a beef cattle venture on this farm where various breeds were raised as an experiment to help determine which might be most adaptive to the climate and the hilly topography of the central mountains. This was done in cooperation with the Agricultural Department of Puerto Rico.

One day someone came running in to say that one of the cows was in trouble. Many of us ran back to the field to check it out and found a hugely bloated cow lying on its side, unable to get up. Enos Nauman, our chief mechanic at the time, took out his big pocket knife, found a specific spot on the animal's back and made an incision through the cow's hide. This let out all the excess foul-smelling gas, like someone emptying an inner tube, until the animal was able to get back on her feet with a little help. I saw this cow a few days later, grazing peacefully among the others, apparently no worse for the wear.

One of the breeds being raised on the farm was called a "Charbroyais," a mix between a Charolais, a French one known as a good meat source, and a Brahman, known as a hearty breed which could thrive in hot, harsh climate conditions. One downside to this mixed type was that the occasional animal seemed to have a mean streak by nature.

One such animal was a particular cow which decided one day to crash through a barbed wire fence and go on a cross-country excursion. When this was discovered, my dad and a number of other Foundation workers gave pursuit, eventually in a variety of vehicles, as the cow wasn't inclined to stay on the farm, but rather headed across hills and valleys on quite a chase. She was finally surrounded what seemed like halfway to La Plata, but not before charging her pursuers. My dad was forced to dive under a fence to avoid her, hitting the side of his head and left ear on a rock. The men finally got several ropes on the animal and forced her on to the back of a high-sided truck, which they had backed up to the side of the hill. Dad sported a fat black-and-blue ear for a while, as a reminder of the incident.

There was quite an assortment of vehicles and machinery on this farm. One was an old Army surplus jeep which was typically parked in a three-sided shed with other Foundation vehicles when not in use. Unique to this jeep was a starter switch mounted on the floor board which engaged the starter motor. When I was a bit older, I discovered that although the jeep would not start without the key in the ignition, this floor-mounted switch would activate the starter motor and turn over the engine. If I put the jeep in reverse and activated the starter, it was powerful enough to turn over the engine and thereby actually back the jeep out of the shed in a chug, chug, chugging motion. Putting the jeep in first gear meant I could return it to its original spot in the shed. I could do this unnoticed if I didn't overdo it to the point the battery went dead. This was my first driving experience.

Explorations on El Monte

There were so many things to explore on this farm. From the citrus orchards to the vegetable-washing vats, from the poultry barns to the building where the eggs were inspected, washed, and graded, and so many more. There were huge stands of bamboo to be explored, trees which yielded mangos and *guamás*, bushes full of *guayabas*, the project ponds used for irrigation, the long irrigation pipes and tractor-powered pump, ravines between the hills and, of course, *El Monte*, the huge hill—a mountain to us as children—which we loved to climb.

That long climb with our neighborhood gang was always an adventure. Near the bottom we would find banana plants, occasionally with ripening fruit which made a tasty snack. Further up, we might find ready-to-eat avocados on a tree. Near the top, we had to avoid the stinging nettles and brambles which made progress difficult. I always loved staring up at the giant tree near the top, with its branches providing a huge canopy, atop which a hawk had a nest. Once at the top of this mountain, one could see for miles across the north and east side of the Island with its succession of mountain ridges all the way to the Atlantic.

The back side of this "mountain" opened onto a grassy hillside with boulders clinging to its side. It was fun to dislodge some of the smaller ones, send them crashing down the steep hillside, and watch them bounce way up in the air, sometimes breaking into smaller pieces on their way to the bottom of the *quebrada* way below. Until one day, a man angrily yelled up at us, telling us we nearly hit his cow at the bottom. The thought had never crossed our minds that we might be putting someone or something in peril.

With the orchards nearby and the multiple types of fruit growing in the wild, it seemed there was always something in season to snack on: guavas, navel oranges, juice oranges, kumquats, *acerolas,* passion fruit, mangos, and the previously mentioned *guamás.* We were always careful to look for worms in the guavas before eating them. Sometimes, as a diversion, we would peel part of the rind off an orange with a knife, bore a hole in the end and suck the juice out while it still hung on the tree.

A Valuable Lesson

In my pre-teen years I developed a love for fishing for largemouth bass, mostly in the project irrigation ponds, but also in the La Plata River if I went along with my dad whenever he made a visit to the Mennonite project in La Plata. Often, while on the river, I would see women come down to the riverside with their baskets of laundry, which they would wash in the river and then pound with paddles on the flat boulders along the river bed.

We always looked forward to visits from the Ulrich family, the benefactors who founded and funded the Foundation. For me, it meant some additional friends to play with, and they always brought interesting gifts or things that weren't otherwise available to us on the Island. Even as a child, I was always impressed by Raymond (Ray) Ulrich's can-do attitude. A successful inventor and businessman, he seemed to find a solution to any problem that presented itself.

A simple example, but one that impressed me significantly as a young fisherman, was something that occurred on a day set aside for recreation during one of the Ulrich family's summer visits. The irrigation pond at the west end of the farm had a healthy population of resident bass, but they were hard to reach due to a heavy growth of reeds along the south edge of the shoreline. Seeing this, Ray cut a bamboo stalk long enough to reach beyond the reeds, attached a piece of fishing line to it, then a lure, and proceeded to walk the shoreline with his lure extending into the water beyond the reeds. To everyone's surprise, he caught fish after fish. In the many times of fishing this pond it had never occurred to me to try this. This seemingly inconsequential activity became a life lesson for me: assess the situation, look at the resources at hand, and determine a way to resolve the problem. It has served me well throughout my career in medical diagnostics development and manufacturing.

Occasional visits to the dairy farm in Asomante, another of the economic development initiatives undertaken by the Ulrich Foundation, presented a whole new set of experiences. It was interesting to watch the cows head into their stalls and the milking machines at work. The tall silo used for silage storage was a fun and somewhat scary place to explore. I can remember running after the small orange parachutes dropped from a single-engine airplane flying over the farm. Attached to these were boxes of dry ice containing bull semen specimens used in the artificial insemination project developed to improve cattle stock. This was the best way to ensure viability of the samples, since in those days the trip from the coast by road could take three hours or more.

Working During my Teen Years

I had a paper route in my early to mid-teen years. I delivered the *San Juan Star*, the only English language newspaper on the Island, to those who preferred to get their news in English. Each morning I would get up at 5:30 a.m. and head downtown to the stairwell behind the pharmacy where the papers were dropped off overnight from the publisher in San Juan. I would sling my paper bag over my shoulder, and ride off on my bicycle on my usual route. It was probably less than five miles long, but seemed like a long route, up and down a few fairly steep climbs across the hills in the Aibonito area.

Dogs were always my biggest concern. My customers preferred to have their paper placed at their front door rather than tossed from the street, where it might land who knows where, exposed to the elements. So, at some homes, I had to enter the fenced yard and deal with their dog. This was usually an uneasy standoff. I would carefully walk by without making any sudden moves. The dogs would limit their aggressiveness to growling and barking. Now, if the owner happened to come out, it was a different story. The dogs would then become more aggressive and charge, I guess to show the owner they were doing their job. This gave the owner the chance to call off the dog, and I would swat at it with my paper in self-defense.

One dog in particular was very aggressive. It was a large German shepherd. When it was in the house, and I approached the front door it would go crazy, knocking over floor lamps and creating quite a ruckus. It only bit me once. One Saturday morning, while collecting my weekly payment, the owner was holding the dog back while we completed the transaction. Unfortunately for me, the dog lunged forward and bit me. Later that weekend, the dog bit one of the owner's children, and the owner gave the dog away to someone else. What a relief!

During my later high school years I had the opportunity to work in the mechanic shop on the Foundation farm in Aibonito during summer break, and to mow lawns around the new Mennonite hospital built in Aibonito. This taught me a lot of practical life skills. By then many of the original Ulrich Foundation projects were winding down, having served their purpose. A concrete mixing plant was set up on Foundation property next to the old chicken barns. This plant was a local source of ready-mix concrete used to build new homes in a subdivision developed on previous Foundation farm property, close to the land donated for the hospital. It also provided the concrete for the town square in Aibonito when it was refurbished. On occasion that summer I would operate a large front-end loader to fill the big hoppers at the concrete plant with sand and gravel.

One day a man came along who wanted to buy a pickup truck load of gravel. I dug into the pile of gravel, filled my front end loader and promptly dumped it into the pickup bed. To my horror, the sudden weight of a full bucket load of gravel into that pickup made it squat almost to the ground. I was sure I had broken the springs under the bed. But the bed bounced back to some extent and, upon inspection, no damage was done. What a relief!

Baseball

We played a number of sports as children, but baseball was king. My experience was mostly limited to pick-up games with neighborhood kids. Once Aibonito Hall was no longer used to house I-W men, my family lived in one end of the house and the Lawrence Greaser family lived in the other end. With four boys in their family and myself, we were allowed to have frequent games of catch in the halls as long as we used a rubber ball to prevent any damage to walls, and such. A favorite pastime of ours on rainy days or evenings after completing homework was to take turns trying to reach from one "base" (usually a rug) to another without being tagged out. These long hallways had slick linoleum floors which made it pretty nice for sliding into base in your sock feet without getting hurt.

I do remember one game I played on an organized team in one of the subsidized housing developments in an Aibonito neighborhood. There were some Little League teams in Aibonito, but my Dad was not in favor of me playing on any of them. On this one occasion, however, I did play as a substitute on one of the teams. I was loaned a team jersey for the game and I felt pretty special. I was taller than most of the players, and fairly rangy, so the coach had me play first base. I thought I played rather well, but having not played on a "real" team before, I wasn't familiar with the established protocol of throwing the ball around the infield after an out was made, before returning it to the pitcher. So, after the first out, rather than throwing the ball "around the horn," I promptly threw the ball to the pitcher. The pitcher, of course, was not expecting the ball, since it would normally be making its way from player to player around the infield. The pitcher was busy leveling out the dirt around the mound with his foot and my tossed ball hit him in the back of the head. He was not pleased, and I was quite embarrassed.

There was a minor league team in Aibonito, which played in a ball park on the outskirts of town. I don't remember going to any of these games as a boy, but I do remember finding a ball in the underbrush behind the outfield fence one time. I did have the opportunity to attend several major league games, however, in the larger cities of Caguas and San Juan. Occasionally someone would take us to watch the professionals play on teams, such as the Criollos de Caguas, Senadores de San Juan, or the Cangrejeros de Santurce which played in the Liga de Béisbol Profesional de Puerto Rico. It was not unusual in those days for major league players from the States to come to Puerto Rico to play on these teams in the winter off-season: I had the privilege of watching players such as Roberto Clemente, Orlando Cepeda, Frank Howard, and Hank Aaron.

Church: A Central Part of our Lives

Both my parents were actively involved in church leadership in many of the young churches. This involved the usual Sunday morning, Sunday evening, and Wednesday evening services, Sunday School classes, Summer Bible School, and specific meetings for men, women, and youth groups. On occasion it included other Sunday afternoon services or special activities during the week. This also involved handling administrative functions of the congregation, and being a local presence in a new church setting to help meet ongoing social and spiritual needs in the community.

At times it meant handing out religious literature in the hope that it would pique an interest in attending some of the church functions or use of the social services provided. Sometimes I would tag along on trips my parents made to San

Juan for business or supplies. We would pass by many homes along the way. Clean running water was mostly available in the island interior by then, but it was not piped into many of the homes. Women and children could be seen along the road carrying water from the closest public outdoor faucet back to their homes in large pots or five-gallon cracker tins repurposed for carrying water—many times balanced on their heads.

On one such occasion, as we passed a woman and her children carrying water, my mother dropped some of the literature out the car window. The woman kneeled down, picked up the literature, and stood back up without losing the tin of water on her head. Mother was delighted. I thought it was quite an athletic feat, but a shame to cause her to do this.

Church was a central part of our life. I was a willing participant in many of these meetings and, as I grew older, served in various roles as Sunday School teacher, head usher, and the like. Church met a lot of social and community needs, as well as spiritual. As a young boy, however, probably 10 to 12 years old by then, Sunday evening prayer meetings became difficult for me to endure. Most of my friends would still be out playing, getting in the last few innings of baseball or some other game before being called in to get ready for evening service. I found it difficult to sit quietly for that long. So before long, I would start timing each person's prayer on my little Timex watch. Then I would see how long I could hold my breath without making a peep. Sorry to say, I'm not sure I contributed much to the group's prayers of praise and supplication, but I did learn patience.

We had an active youth group and enjoyed a lot of activities together. Occasionally we would go on a sponsored trip to one of the beaches for the day, which was always fun. At Christmastime we enjoyed caroling or singing traditional Puerto Rican *aguinaldos* with our guitars, *güiros*, and maracas while we travelled from house to house as *parranderos*. We were often invited in for traditional Spanish butter cookies, *café con leche*, or *ponche* (eggnog). Of course we were served the non-alcoholic version.

Often a group of us would enjoy walking downtown after Sunday evening service to the bakery where fresh bread was baking for Monday morning. As we drew near, we could smell the wonderful baked bread aroma carried down the street by the evening breeze. Arriving at the bakery, we would watch as the loaves were moved around in the huge oven by the baker, using a big flat wooden spatula with a very long handle. We would buy a long loaf of *pan de agua* or *pan de manteca* fresh out of the oven and share it on our way back to the church.

An Unexpected Joyride

One evening after church one of the *jóvenes* who was old enough to have a driver's license borrowed his dad's car with the intent of taking one of our friends home to La Plata. A number of us boys piled in to go along. However, rather than go straight to La Plata, someone suggested we first go to Coamo to enjoy the *Fiestas Patronales* there.

Now, having been a Spanish colony for nearly four centuries, Puerto Rico was steeped in Spanish traditions, and predominantly Catholic. So each town had its own patron saint, and once a year this saint was honored with a religious procession, followed by a week of festivities on the town square. This included Ferris wheel rides and such for the children, and music and dancing and merriment for all. Each night there was a display of fireworks. Since this was a primarily Catholic tradition, and included activities not deemed appropriate for a conservative Mennonite, it was frowned upon in our household. So I never went to the *Fiestas Patronales* in Aibonito. We would, however, watch the fireworks display from our balcony at Aibonito Hall, a half mile away.

So it was that on this particular evening, our carload of young teenagers set out to experience the *Fiestas Patronales* in Coamo before going to La Plata—a half hour away in totally the opposite direction. Now, Aibonito is in the mountains, and

Coamo is at the foot of the central mountains, closer to the flat southern coast. The road from Aibonito to Coamo traverses the steep mountainside, with many switchbacks and cliffs over which an occasional vehicle would plunge. It was not uncommon to see a white cross marking the spot along the roadside where some unfortunate traveler rode the cliff to their death.

From Aibonito we had made it through Asomante and were negotiating the steep switchbacks toward Coamo, when suddenly the rear axle on the car broke. One of the wheels popped out of place, severed one of the brake fluid lines, and quickly left the car with very little braking power. It now felt like we were on a roller coaster as the driver did his best to negotiate the curves with what seemed like a runaway car. It was white-knuckle time till we negotiated the bridge across the river at the base of the mountain, and coasted safely to a stop. I don't remember how we got home, or what the punishment was for our little adventure, if there even was a punishment. I do know we never made it to the *Fiestas Patronales* in Coamo. But we did get our joyride.

School Years in Aibonito

My formal education started in kindergarten held at the Methodist Church in downtown Aibonito. Nothing memorable of this year stands out for me, except for the graduation ceremony. For it, we all were decked out in all-white outfits, right down to white shoes. After graduation my mother stained them brown so I could get some use out of them.

I attended Escuela Betania in Pulguillas for grades one through nine, except for second grade, when we spent the year on furlough in Roanoke, Illinois. This was my first exposure to a winter and snow in the Midwest. I enjoyed sledding down one of the streets, which had a decent grade to it and could get rather icy. It was ideal for sledding as long as no cars were on the road.

It was also my first exposure to a fire escape. Our classroom was on second floor. I was a bit scared, the first time during a fire drill, when I was asked to jump into the dark tube and slide down to the playground below.

The other school incident I remember occurred as we were lined up in the hallway to go home for Christmas break. We had all enjoyed a party with sweets and goodies at the end of the day. Unfortunately for me, the boy behind me must have over-indulged on candy, cookies, and milk. He got sick, and the back of my winter coat became his target. As soon as I got outside I jumped in a snow bank and slid on my back to get the worst of the regurgitated mess off my coat. This, of course, was great entertainment for the school kids streaming out the door. It was not a pleasant walk home that day.

Back in Puerto Rico, third grade was a year of reconnecting and enjoying the year-round mild temperatures. As there was only one class at each grade level, we enjoyed the same core of classmates all the way through ninth grade.

A large group of students heading for Betania School would wait for the bus along the main road, Route 14, either at the base of the hill at Aibonito Hall or in front of the Banco Popular in downtown Aibonito, depending on where we lived at the time. I can remember one rare occasion when it was cool enough I could see my breath in the morning air while waiting for the bus. Usually, however, the only inconvenience might be a stray rain shower from which to take shelter.

The yellow school bus would wind its way up from La Plata, through Aibonito, then through Asomante, picking up students along the way. From Coamo and other starting points, large covered flatbed trucks, fitted with wooden bench seats along the sides of the bed—similar to troop carriers—, would also make their way to Betania School in Pulguillas, picking up students from designated stops along the road.

Third through ninth grades were mostly pleasant school years. Quality instruction was provided by dedicated teachers. All classes were conducted in Spanish, except for one English class each day. Noon meals were always provided and included government-subsidized dried and packaged food. We had a lot of rice and beans, which I really liked, reconstituted eggs and canned corn, which were not favorites of mine, and powdered milk, which I and many others really disliked. We were allowed to bring powdered chocolate or strawberry flavoring from home to make the milk more palatable. On rare occasions we might find a small white worm which had found its way into the bulk box of powdered milk and happened to end up in one of our glasses. If you were the lucky one, you were excused from drinking your milk that day.

Our third grade teacher's preferred method of maintaining discipline was to throw chalk or erasers at anyone who got out of line during class. The fourth grade teacher preferred to have us kneel in a corner at the front of the class while holding a stack of books in each hand, similar to how a waiter might hold a tray next to his head. If someone really misbehaved, they might get a couple of stout yardstick licks across the back of the calves. I don't really remember any other forms of punishment over the years, either because they were less memorable, or because we had all learned to behave by then.

In sixth or seventh grade, I don't exactly remember when, Mother thought it would be a good idea if I learned to play the piano. She enjoyed playing, and thought I might as well. So I took piano lessons for a couple of years from an English teacher who came to Puerto Rico to serve in Mennonite Voluntary Service. She was also a very good piano teacher. I must say I never took a liking to piano playing.

Each day I would practice for a half hour. I would watch out the window as my friends were playing in the yard and I was going through my scales or stumbling through a rudimentary version of "My Bonnie Lies Over the Ocean." Sometimes I would practice mornings before school until the kids waiting for the bus down the hill would yell up "¡Aquí viene la guagua!," and I would grab my books and run down to get on the bus. Finally, after struggling through yet another lesson, my frustrated teacher suggested piano playing might not be suited to me. I was happy to agree with her, and I guess my mother concurred.

I attended tenth grade in the public high school in Aibonito. It was an easy walk, slightly over a half mile to school from our house. This was a much larger school than Betania. My history and social studies class was just before lunch. Our teacher in this class would give me some money each day, and ask me to go down the street to get him *empanadas* or *rellenos* for his lunch. This was nice in that it gave me a break from the classroom, but it meant I didn't get much out of the day's lesson. I had to make sure I studied my textbook closely at home so I could still succeed at test time.

Broadening Opportunities in Santurce

By then my folks decided, rightly so, that I needed additional schooling in English, so I wouldn't struggle in college in the States. For my last two years of high school I attended Robinson School, sponsored by the Methodist church, in Santurce, which is part of the larger San Juan metropolis. This brought with it new challenges. During the week I lived with a Mennonite family who had an extra bedroom, and on weekends I would return to Aibonito. The first few months my folks would bring me in to San Juan for the week and pick me up Friday evenings. Each school day the man whose family I stayed with would drop me off on his way to work.

Evenings, however, his schedule and mine didn't coincide, so I needed to find my own way home. Santurce is a considerable distance across the city from where they lived in Bayamón. I was vaguely familiar with the city, but didn't know my way around, and certainly didn't know the bus schedule, or the routes to get back home. It was quite an adventure getting home the first week. I would wait at a bus stop till I saw a bus with a marquee indicating it was going somewhere in the general direction I needed to go. And I would ask others waiting at the bus stops about which buses went a particular way. If the bus then headed in a direction away from my destination, I would get off at the next stop and wait for another bus that looked right. The first night, I got to a shopping center I recognized as being close to my adopted family's house, and took a taxi home from there. It took me several days of trial and error till I discovered a bus that went right through the subdivision where I lived. Then it took me only a couple of bus transfers each night to get home.

Within a couple of months my folks bought me a car, which made getting back and forth to school, and the weekend trips to Aibonito, much easier for everyone. This car was a small 1964 MG sedan, not as well-known as the convertible roadsters, but still a fun car to drive, and well suited to the winding roads between Aibonito and the city. We purchased the car from a Robinson classmate of mine at a reasonable price, not knowing, however, that he had run it rather hard before we purchased it. These cars, while a blast to drive, were not very reliable. I probably was not that easy on it myself. It needed a significant amount of maintenance and repair from time to time. Luckily, I had access to the mechanic shop at the Ulrich Foundation and a father who was very knowledgeable. We spent quite a few hours together working on this car. It was a good learning opportunity for me and a great bonding experience for us.

For the first time I had the opportunity to play organized varsity sports at Robinson School. We played football, basketball, and baseball against schools from the military bases on the Island and teams from other church-related private schools in the area. Most of the military base schools were larger than ours, so they were always a challenge to compete against. We played our home football games in the old Sixto Escobar baseball stadium, which by then had been abandoned in favor of the new Hiram Bithorn stadium, named in honor of the first Puerto Rican to play in the major leagues. Bithorn first played for the Cubs in 1942. I felt honored to play on the same field where I had watched baseball heroes play only a few years earlier, even though it was a different sport, and the stands contained only a tiny fraction of the fans who previously attended the baseball games.

This school did in fact help prepare me for college. Spanish was still my first language when it came to writing, and essay writing in general was a challenge. I remember how embarrassed I was the day my English composition teacher read one of my early essays to the class as an example of how not to write an essay. He didn't reveal my name, but I felt all eyes on me as he read. I learned a lot from him on how to express myself convincingly, and my English vocabulary increased significantly.

Since Robinson was a church-sponsored school, a religion class was always part of the curriculum. One of these classes explored many religions and different denominations of the Christian faith. On one occasion I had the opportunity to invite Dave Helmuth, then the pastor at the Mennonite church in San Juan, to tell our class about Mennonites. My classmates were primarily from Catholic, Jewish, or one of the mainstream Protestant faith backgrounds. The Mennonite peace stand and our opposition to participation in the military were totally foreign to them. Later, Dave commented to me how confrontational that classroom experience was that day. True, but that class opened my thinking to be more acceptant of other's religious views, and to see religious faith in ways not previously seen.

Living away from home at sixteen and being thrust into city life and a new, and sometimes hostile environment, after growing up in such a supportive and nurturing setting, was difficult, but it was very critical to my growth and development. It opened my eyes to new ideas and helped me learn how to deal with challenges from a broader perspective.

Grateful for my Life on the Island

After leaving for college that August afternoon in 1968, I never did return to live in Puerto Rico. I've made short term visits back on several occasions for business or pleasure. On one trip

I had the opportunity to take my wife and both my daughters on a brief tour of the general area where I grew up. We visited the old Aibonito Hall, which at that time was abandoned. I was saddened by what I saw. The front double doors were wide open and the house was in such disrepair I didn't venture in beyond the front vestibule. The grand house was a shell of its former self. It no longer had any of the vibrant life I had known as a child. I am delighted that Linda Ulrich Nussbaum, daughter of Ray and Verda Ulrich, and her husband Harry have since directed a project which has completely restored this home to its original glory, and repurposed it to again serve the community.

I feel very blessed having grown up as a Mennonite in Puerto Rico, and for the exposure to a diversity of cultures, ideas, and experiences which this afforded me. My life would be much different had my parents not answered the call to serve in Puerto Rico. While life then had its challenges, it was also abundantly rewarding.

There has been tremendous change in Puerto Rico since those years in the 1950s and 1960s. Roads are vastly improved, with superhighways which cut the travel time from San Juan to Aibonito from nearly three hours to just over an hour. Aibonito itself has grown to the point where much of the past is barely recognizable. The Mennonite Hospital has grown to a multi-site organization serving over 300,000 patients a year. Both Academia Mennonita Betania in Puguillas and Academia Menonita de Summit Hills in the metropolitan area continue to provide quality education for many students. Many of the early projects have developed, directly or indirectly, into successful business enterprises.

It is rewarding to feel, in a small way, a part of an endeavor which brought about positive change. While things are vastly different in Puerto Rico now than then, the memories remain. I will always cherish my youth in *"La Isla del Encanto."*

Chapter 9

MY PUERTO RICAN INTERCULTURAL FAITH FOUNDATIONS

Ruth Kaufman Strube

Once upon a time in the small Caribbean island of Puerto Rico, there was a beautiful young woman named Providencia Carrasquillo Sánchez. Provi was born in Luquillo in 1926. She and her younger sister were raised in Fajardo, mostly by her mother and grandmother. Around the mid-1940s, with her family now living in Cayey, Provi rode the public transportation to La Plata to train as a nurse aide in the Hospital General Menonita. After completion of her studies, she worked at the Hospital, as well as with dentist Earl Stover.

Orvin Kaufman was born in 1916 in LaGrange, Indiana. He contracted polio at the age of eight or nine, and walked with a limp. Arriving in La Plata in August 1948, Orvin worked at the same hospital as Provi during a two-year assignment. He was a talented mechanic, electrician, and skilled refrigeration technician, and learned there to read and write in Spanish. Dad eventually lived in Puerto Rico for 22 years—he loved the weather and the people.

After his two-year term was up, since there was no one to replace Orvin, he was asked if he could stay longer. He agreed. By then Orvin and Provi, my parents, were seeing each other. Mennonite worker John Brandeberry and others had been used by God to help my dad notice my mom. Orvin was shy, so they had encouraged him to go out with her. It worked! Remember the song in the movie *Fiddler on the Roof?* It goes like this, "Matchmaker, Matchmaker, make me a match...". When Dad's replacement finally came, my parents were already engaged and then got married on November 27, 1950 in Cayey.

Our Family Begins

Orvin and Provi lived in a two-family house at the Ulrich Foundation farm near Aibonito. To this union were born Jimmy, a still-born daughter Susie, and twins Ruthie and Edith. Later Dad had a nice cement house built in barrio Asomante up on the hilltop overlooking a public housing development known as *las parcelas*, and the island of Caja de Muertos in the Caribbean Sea.

I remember him telling a story about this three-bedroom house. While it was being built, Mami wondered why he wanted such a big place since Jimmy was the only child. Well, God has a sense of humor—unexpected twins were born in January 1956. Full house! I say "unexpected twins" because when my parents asked the doctor if Mami was going to have twins, he thought it was just one baby. When the time came, I was born first, and 32 minutes later, Edith arrived. If my parents were alive now, I would ask them how they managed, in such a short time, to provide for an extra baby. I am sure that their family and friends reached out to help. I know that my Puerto Rican grandmother Vicenta Sánchez Pérez, whom we called Mama Nene, helped care for us that first year. Mami was a stay-at-home mom. This provided security and stability in our home. Dad was self-employed.

Here let me also tell you about the little car my father drove for twenty-two years: a gray 1952 Morris Minor with a manual transmission. He did the repairs himself. What people remember most about this car were the turn signals. They were little yellow arms, one on each side, that popped out of the door when the turn signal switch was activated. When children saw

Dad's car going down the road, they would yell, "*saca la manita*" (stick out the little hand). Everyone got a good chuckle out of it!

Edith and I weren't old enough to drive on the road, but we took turns sitting on his lap, steering the car down our lane while he maneuvered the foot pedals. We learned to use the stick shift. Dad taught Mami to drive this car. I can still hear him telling her to shift when going up a hill, because she waited too long. This was a five-passenger car. I believe we squeezed eight or nine people in it on the way to church.

Nurturing Faith

Dad was raised Mennonite and Mami was raised Baptist. They both had a personal relationship with Jesus as their Savior and Lord. After they got married, they attended the Mennonite church in Pulguillas. My parents were my role models. They taught us children by example: how to pray, have daily Bible reading, attend church regularly, serve in the church, worship the true and living God, help others, share our faith, do good works, and to stay away from worldly places that could corrupt our moral values. My brother Jim told me once that when he was ready to settle down and get married, he wanted a Christian home like Dad and Mom's. He has that now.

As a family, we were regular church attenders. Sunday was a day of rest and church attendance. We were taught to give: tithes, offerings, and alms to the poor. To this day, it's not hard to do these things. I've discovered the joy of obeying God and giving.

There was a time when we attended the Mennonite church in Usabón to be of help and support for this small congregation. I remember the Raúl and María Luisa Espada family with lots of children, around 12 at that time. I was impressed to hear how the older children helped with their younger siblings. I recall my mother reading us a missionary story in front of that church. I liked looking at the pictures. All I remember of the story is that an *amuleto* (amulet, charm) doesn't have the power to protect a person, but God does.

I enjoyed attending Sunday School and Wednesday evening classes in Pulguillas. Our teachers taught us Bible stories and lots of songs. I had fun coloring pictures related to the lesson and doing crafts. Once in a while on Wednesdays we played in the school playground.

One of my friends shared her box of dry jello with me. We wet our finger, dipped it in the jello mix, and licked it. It was sweet! Our finger turned red. Remember that, Ruthie Miller? A happy memory! Not just the sweet treat, but the good friendships that were cultivated in a Christian environment. While parents were visiting after church, we would slide down a small hill on a palm tree leaf that had dropped. Who needs snow and a sled? It was fun!

When there wasn't a class for the children, we would sit in church with our parents. If we didn't behave ourselves, Dad would have Edith and me sit between him and Mami, thump us on the head, or take us outside. Then back into the service we went. Discipline was a part of our upbringing. It didn't warp our personality. We were taught submission to authority and self-control. There was love, joy, and peace in our home and our lives.

Vacation Bible School was also a fun time. I still have a craft project I made, a wall plaque made of plaster of Paris with the verse, *"Dios es nuestro amparo y fortaleza" Salmo 46:1a* ("God is our refuge and strength" Psalm 46:1a).

Being "born again"—saved through faith in Jesus—was another experience. Mami said I accepted Jesus as my Savior when I was real young, though I don't remember the exact age nor the place. I have loved God and Jesus all my life. I feel like I have been a Christian forever. Yet, as I matured, I realized that I could not get to heaven on my parents' salvation experience.

One day I walked outside to the back of my house to talk to God. I said something like I mentioned above and that I wanted to go to heaven someday. I asked God to forgive my sins and invited Jesus into my heart. Then I went back into the house. I had made my peace with God. I had the assurance of my salvation because I obeyed God's word. I remember being baptized by sprinkling at the Pulguillas church and got to wear my head covering (*mantilla*) during the services.

In June 1967 when the Billy Graham Evangelistic team came to the Hiram Bithorn Stadium in San Juan, Puerto Rico, my sister and I rededicated our lives to Jesus. I wanted everyone there to know that Jesus was my Savior and my life was His forever. I still have the booklet from the crusade. Then on September 23, 1971, I was baptized by immersion in Toowoomba, Queensland, Australia, where my parents, Edith, and I lived for a short time.

My School

The school and church we attended were in Pulguillas. My first grade teacher was Sra. Rose Fuentes. She taught our class a song about a little bird who was singing on a tree branch. The bird was happy because she had a nest. Sra. Fuentes chose a student to hold a tree branch in front of the classroom, and sing the bird's solo part. Here are the words in Spanish:

Class: *En la rama verde hay un pajarito. Canta así*:
Bird: *Tweet, tweet, tweet.*
Class: *Tiene un nidito, un nidito allí.*
Bird: *Tweet, tweet, tweet, tweet, tweet.*
Class: *Dime, pajarito, dime ya. ¿Pór que siempre estás alegre allá?*
Bird: *Porque tengo un nido, un nidito allí. Tweet, tweet, tweet, tweet, tweet.*

Then she would choose another student to stand in front of the class, hold the tree branch and sing the solo part. I really liked that song. I reminded Sra. Fuentes about this song while attending a Puerto Rican Mennonite reunion in Indiana in 2013. She joined me in singing it. Priceless!

Jimmy, Edith, and I rode the school bus. One of our bus drivers was also a teacher, Sr. Royal Snyder of La Plata. As an adult now, I realize how much time he spent with children. That was a big sacrifice on his part, and a labor of love. He is one of

many Mennonites who worked tirelessly for the cause of Christ.
Thank you! ¡*Gracias*!

Betania was a place where we were taught about God, the
Creator. The teachings in the Bible were our guide to live by.
The staff was a good example to us students. Discipline was
used to discourage bad behavior, and encourage us to do what
was right by God's standards. We received a well-balanced
education. I enjoyed having Puerto Rican and American
teachers and workers to interact with.

The Academia Menonita Betania had an outdoor swimming
pool that we used for physical education class. That is where I
learned to swim. We also played softball, volleyball, and
basketball on the outdoor *cancha*. Track and field day was fun
because we got out of class and competed with our classmates.
We ran and ran and ran until we were exhausted. We laughed,
cheered, yelled, got hot and sweaty, ate, and the winners
received ribbons.

Another class I enjoyed was Home Economics. We learned
practical things like cooking, and sewing on a foot treadle
sewing machine. I learned to make my own patterns from
scratch. That was interesting. I never used that skill again, but I
did take Home Economics in high school and continued
learning.

Sra. Leah Liechty taught us how to bake and decorate
cakes. I made nice-looking petal flowers with frosting, using
powdered sugar and shortening, and learned the trick to frosting
a cake without lines. After frosting the cake, wet your spreading
knife with water and smooth out the lines.

Music class with Srta. Alicia Kehl was fun. I learned many
choruses and songs. Some were taken right out of the Bible. So
God's words were hidden in our hearts. She played the
accordion really well. Another teacher taught us to play the
recorder. One year I took piano lessons. Since we didn't have a
piano at home, it was difficult to practice. I use to ride my
bicycle to Stanley and Fern Miller's house to practice piano. I
quit after that year.

Now I wish that I would have made the effort to take music classes in high school because at this point in my life I love music, to worship the Lord. When I was younger I was shy, so that's why I didn't do many things. I liked working behind the scene better. My twin was the leader, and I followed. Later, in my early 20s, I joined a large church choir in Fort Wayne, Indiana. I didn't even have to audition,—thank you, Jesus! That was how I learned more about music and found out that I have a passion for it. The Lord set me free to worship Him in front of hundreds of people.

Back to my experiences at Betania. What is a school without a *comedor* (lunchroom)? I looked forward to eating lunch— except for cooked spinach. To this day I will not eat it cooked. I am thankful that I was used to drinking powdered milk at home because at school, that's what they served...warm powdered milk. Once in a while, the supervisor of the schools showed up at lunch time. That meant that we had to eat our food and waste less. So if we didn't like something, we tried to trade with someone near us. I can't speak for my sister but I remember drinking more than one glass of milk in order to help out a fellow classmate. Ha, ha, ha. The silly things one remembers from the past. Do you remember eating *pegao?* That's the rice that got burnt in the bottom of the pan. It was crispy and greasy. The cooks let us know if we could have seconds on the rice. Yummy! *Gracias, cocineras,* for lovingly preparing our lunches.

A Multi-Cultural Environment

Special memories from those years in Puerto Rico include the typical foods and Island traditions. I enjoyed foods like fresh tropical fruits, *pasteles, arroz con dulce,* guava paste with Colby cheese, and especially sucking juice from a sugarcane stalk. There were also *bacalaítos,* codfish with vegetables, and other foods whose names I can't remember. And Christmas celebrations, singing songs and eating tasty foods, like *lechón asado,* are memorable.

One of my unforgettable experiences was when Edith and I played with Nelly, our Catholic neighbor. It didn't matter that she was of a different faith. Our families were welcomed into each other's homes. I saw how they lived. Sometimes Doña Luisa, my neighbor, gave me rice with fried eggs. Delicious!

Mami had an electric washing machine; Doña Luisa didn't. I wanted to experience the way she did her laundry. Sometimes I asked her if I could do their laundry. She had a big round tub outdoors full of water with clothes soaking in it. I used the bar of soap and a washboard to wash the clothes, then rinsed them in another tub. Finally, the clothes were hung up to dry on a clothesline. I got to see both cultures live and work side by side. We learned to respect the differences yet hold fast to our Mennonite teachings.

I don't remember the year we got a television in the house, probably in the late 1960s. We enjoyed watching it. Mami sometimes had a hard time getting Edith and me to do our chores first. We never did have a telephone at home in Puerto Rico.

Because of the many Americans on the Island, there were lots of mixed marriages. One weekend, the mixed-marriage families had an outing at Boquerón Beach in Cabo Rojo. We stayed in cabins. Many of us kids got sunburned; we looked like red lobsters. Another enjoyable experience for me was going to the Aibonito Mennonite church one Sunday evening for an English hymn sing. Boy, could they harmonize!

Leaving Puerto Rico

Jimmy graduated from Betania in 1967. He attended half a semester at Caribbean Grace Academy, between Santa Isabel and Ponce, until it was closed. Then he finished 10th grade in Aibonito before moving to Middlebury, Indiana, to live with relatives. When he graduated from Northridge High School in 1970, Mami, Edith, and I flew up for his graduation. Dad couldn't come because he had a house to sell and had to get a lot of things packed. It took several months, but when it was bought by Paul and Ruth Miller, a Mennonite couple who lived down the road from us, he was finally able to arrive in Middlebury.

It had been my dad's ambition to someday live in Queensland, Australia where there was more room to live. Puerto Rico was overpopulated, and my uncle Roy had pointed out to Dad the benefits of living in Australia. So Dad started to read up about it, and decided a few years later to move there. That dream came true for us in August 1971. Jim didn't go with us; he was living on his own then. All our material possessions were packed in nine big barrels.

For various reasons, including the fact that Edith and I had missed two years of school in our moves, we returned to Indiana six weeks later and started high school. Later, while living in North Webster, Indiana, we finally decided to unpack these barrels. It was like Christmas in the middle of summer. There were a lot of memories in there. Can you imagine having to work all day, come home, fix supper for one, then go through all the house contents and guess who wants what, and decide whether to pack it, give it away, sell it, or toss it?

Family Update

Dad passed away in March 1994 in Warsaw, Indiana, and Mami in September 2014 in Anderson, South Carolina. They are buried in Middlebury, Indiana. Jim and his family live in Anderson, South Carolina. Edith Velázquez and her family live near Fort Wayne, Indiana. My husband and I live in Ottumwa, Iowa. We are all serving the Lord in our local churches, and continue to use the Spanish language wherever needed. My husband Chris and I attend a weekly Spanish Bible study class and enjoy the fellowship with my Hispanic brothers and sisters in Christ. It reminds me of my roots.

Final Thoughts

I want to thank the Mennonites who obeyed the call of God and went to Puerto Rico with the gospel of Jesus Christ. They were missionaries, pastors, teachers, volunteer servants, doctors, nurses, radio broadcasters, farmers, mechanics, electricians, secretaries, administrators, and others. They left the comforts of North America, or other countries, to invest in a poor island. Their presence and contribution has changed the Island and the lives of its people. Thanks to those who gave of their resources for the cause.

Many Puerto Ricans came on board with what God was doing on the Island. They went to seminary to become pastors and leaders. Others received on-the-job training, and became skillful in their fields. It has been nice to see two cultures become as one. I thank God for His guidance, wisdom, and knowledge in orchestrating this whole project.

I am very thankful for my Christian heritage, and for the foundation that was taught at home, church, and school. Jesus Christ is the Solid Rock on which my life is built. He has saved me when the storms of life have come. I am rooted in Him. My husband and I have passed that Christian heritage on to our four children. We have seen the benefits of Christian education so we have made that a priority for our family. I have learned that in life one must choose to follow God and make that a priority. If not, there are plenty of distractions in the world that will lure us away from Him. "But as for me and my house, we will serve the Lord" (Joshua 24:15).

Chapter 10

I FOUND MY TRUE LOVE IN PUERTO RICO

Rolando Santiago

Raquel's mother, Doña Modesta Martínez, enjoyed telling the story that she and my mother Patricia saw each other when both Raquel and I were growing in their wombs in Puerto Rico. She implied that before birth, Raquel and I had already been in close proximity to each other.

Early Connections

My first awareness of Raquel was when she came to La Plata as a child to visit her sister Irma, who was the wife of my pastor, Raúl Rosado. I remember seeing Raquel in vacation Bible school classes. At that time, I enjoyed her presence, but not more than any other classmate in vacation Bible classes.

My family took a three-week trip to the United States in the summer of 1969 to visit my grandparents, Tim and Rowena Brenneman, in Goshen, Indiana. On a side trip, we visited my aunt Elisa Santiago in New York City. By that time, Raquel and her mother had relocated to the South Bronx from the rural community of Guavate in the east central mountains of Puerto Rico. Our family also paid a visit to Doña Modesta in her Bronx apartment. I remember seeing Raquel in the apartment, but I don't remember talking with her. Raquel and I would have been 12 years old at the time.

I left home in early August of 1974 to enroll at Eastern Mennonite High School for my final year of high school. I felt I needed a full year of English instruction to prepare for coursework at a Mennonite college in the United States. Most of my elementary and secondary schooling had been in Spanish. I was 17 at the time. I missed my friends in Puerto Rico.

I was determined to visit Puerto Rico annually during my undergraduate years at Eastern Mennonite College. I did so in most Christmas seasons. Raquel was on the Island during that time. She was attending Catholic University of America in the southern city of Ponce, working on a bachelor's degree in nursing. I would travel with friends from the La Plata Mennonite congregation to visit friends in the Ponce Mennonite congregation. Raquel was part of the youth group of the Ponce congregation, led by missionary Gladys Widmer. Raquel and I were acquainted with each other, but we had not had opportunities to talk with each other in our youth.

During the summer session of 1979 at Eastern Mennonite College, I was taking my last two courses for my bachelor's degree in psychology. I received a copy of the latest *Alcance Menonita*, the bimonthly newsletter of the Mennonite churches in Puerto Rico. In the issue, there was a lovely graduation photo of Raquel. She looked stunning. How could a simple image of a young woman with penetrating dark eyes, lively black curls, and an authentic smile, who was only an acquaintance, speak to my heart, and urge me to get to know her better?

Time Alone With Raquel

My first opportunity to befriend Raquel at a personal level was at the Mennonite General Assembly in Waterloo, Ontario, August 11-16, 1979. Vicky Colón, a mutual friend, told me that she and Raquel were coming to Waterloo. They were part of a young adult delegation from the Convention of Mennonite Evangelical Churches of Puerto Rico. I was also planning to attend. I had been invited to give a response to one of the sermons at the Assembly. I remember spending time with Vicky, Raquel, and the rest of the Puerto Rican young adult delegation. But there was hardly any time for Raquel and me to talk with each other alone. Our one-on-one conversations would have to wait for another day.

In early September of 1979, I started full-time employment as the assistant director of the U.S. Program of Mennonite Central Committee in Akron, Pennsylvania. Raquel began to work as a full-time staff nurse at the Mennonite General Hospital in Aibonito, Puerto Rico. As I had done during the college years, I requested vacation time in Puerto Rico during the Christmas season. I especially wanted to attend the week-long youth retreat of the Puerto Rico Mennonite Evangelical Youth, the youth organization known for many years as the Juventud Evangélica Menonita Puertorriqueña, or JEMP.

I arrived on the Island about two weeks before the early January JEMP retreat. I stayed at my parents' home in La Plata. My brother Richard who was one-and-a-half years younger than me was also living at home. Richard and I had bonded after our teenage years. He became my best friend. He attended the Aibonito Mennonite Church with my parents, the same church Raquel attended. Richard was a good friend of Raquel. They both shared a personality trait to keep life light and fun, and not take it too seriously. Richard was patient with me when I asked him question after question about Raquel. The more he shared, the more I was attracted to Raquel.

One evening, the Aibonito congregation planned to sing Christmas carols at various homes in the community. I joined the group. Raquel also joined. One of our stops was at the home of Armando and Eunice Hernández in La Sierra, a mountain range a couple of miles south from the town of Aibonito along the Puerto Rico Panoramic Route. After caroling and eating delicious Christmas treats, Raquel and I found a quiet place in the kitchen. At last she and I were able to talk, without anyone else around us. The minutes ticked away. Our souls connected. But all too soon, the leader of the caroling group interrupted us to announce the next stop.

The day for the January JEMP retreat arrived. It took place in a Pentecostal retreat center outside the town of Cidra. I looked forward to it. Raquel would be there. I would have more chances to interact with her. However, as it often happened in church retreats, the young adults spent their time mostly in groups. Raquel and I did the same. If I was going to get her attention, I would have to do it among others during a Bible study, listening to a speaker, enjoying a meal time, playing games, or simply hanging out.

One time, I found myself hanging out with others in the courtyard. I picked up pebbles from the ground. While I talked with her and with others in the group, I started to throw pebbles mindlessly at her. I caught her attention. She understood what I was doing—throwing hints of affection her way. Next thing, Raquel and I exchanged addresses. We committed to writing to each other. This was good enough for me, a major accomplishment, especially when I found out later that I was not the only guy courting her at the retreat.

The next day I flew back to the United States. It did not take a day back in Lancaster, Pennsylvania, and I was already writing a letter to Raquel. Soon after, I received Raquel's response. Then I sent another letter. She responded immediately. I noticed the quick turnaround. So I sent letters more frequently, sensing that Raquel would respond in kind. And she did.

The letters were about events in my life. They described my likes and dislikes. They especially showed my opinions, like my love for Puerto Rico and its culture. I quoted poems by Julia de Burgos, a popular Puerto Rican poet.

It didn't take me long to request more vacation time from Mennonite Central Committee. My feelings of love toward Raquel were bursting through my heart. However, it would have been wrong to ask her to be my girlfriend through letters. I had to do it in person. To get approval for a two-week vacation in the summer of 1980, I took a leave of absence without pay. I booked a flight for early July.

Unexpected Occurence

The phone rang at my office in Akron. The call was from Puerto Rico. My father told me that Richard had been in a terrible accident. He was unconscious with a head injury at the Centro Médico in Río Piedras. It was late June, about a week and a half before my scheduled vacation.

I immediately booked a flight to the Island. I re-arranged my travel plans, but kept intact the two weeks of unpaid vacation I had requested.

The first person who greeted me in the hallway at Centro Médico was Becky Rivera. She was a long-time neighbor from La Plata who grew up with her parents Esteban and Neida Rivera and her sister Betsy in a house across the road from my family's house. She was about three years older than I. Our families were close. Becky was like a big sister to me. When I saw her at Centro Médico, I finally broke down and cried. At that moment, in her consoling arms, Becky was the only one who understood my mixed emotions of fear for Richard's life and my deep love for him.

Richard died two days later. Our family made the necessary funeral arrangements. The viewing took place in our home in La Plata for two consecutive days and nights. And then we had the memorial service. It took place in the Mennonite church in La Plata, known as Iglesia Evangélica Menonita del Calvario. This was the church where Richard and I grew up. I gave the eulogy. I told friends, church members, and my family to celebrate Richard's life and be grateful to God for the gift Richard had been to us during the 21 years he spent with us on earth.

Richard had been part of a Dodge Colt club in La Plata. Club members asked the municipal police department of Aibonito to allow them to remove the "headers" from their car engines when they processed through town toward the town's cemetery. The police department granted the request. The sound of the unprotected mufflers bounced loudly back and forth from wall to wall across stores and residences lining the main street of Aibonito. It felt like a hymn of many trumpets, celebrating Richard's joyous life on earth, as it would be in heaven.

The burial was complete.

Time for the Big Question

I had one week of vacation left in Puerto Rico, and a new chapter in my life was about to begin.

I knocked on the door of Irma and Raúl's house in Aibonito. It was the day after Richard's memorial service. Irma opened the door. She welcomed me. She invited me to sit at the kitchen table. She offered me coffee. I asked if Raúl was home. I said I was interested in speaking with him about Mennonite church life in Puerto Rico, and my work at the Mennonite Central Committee, topics of mutual interest to him and me.

But Irma knew. My primary goal was to speak with Raquel. It was obvious. The many letters I sent to Raquel had come to Irma's house. She had seen the letters.

Raquel was in her bedroom. She did not come out. She was asleep. She had worked at the hospital the night before. Raúl was not at home either. So, Irma and I agreed I should come back the next day.

I returned the following day, and spent the afternoon at Irma and Raúl's place. Raquel was also available. The whole Rosado family, with Raquel and I, gathered around the table. Raquel and I were happy to see each other after months of prolific correspondence.

In the late afternoon, it was time for the youth in the family to go to a meeting of the young adult group at Aibonito Mennonite Church. Charlie Rosado, unrelated to Irma and Raúl, offered to drive Raquel's three nieces to the meeting. I offered to take Raquel in my car. She assented. She and I were nervous. Our relationship had grown through letter writing, not by seeing each other in person. Once in the car, I told Raquel, "let's skip the youth meeting and go eat pizza." I asked her, "would you go with me?" Without hesitation, she agreed. Our pizzeria of choice was located in Cayey, a neighboring town about 20 minutes away.

We had a lovely conversation. After a five-month period of writing to each other, we each knew that the moment had come for me to tell her face-to-face that I loved her. I went to the point, "I love you very much, Raquel. Will you be my girlfriend?" In Spanish, the word for girlfriend is "*novia*." Both in English and in Spanish, the words "girlfriend" and "*novia*" connote a desire for a romantic relationship. Raquel hesitated to give an answer that evening. In fact, she hesitated for two or three days. The waiting period was unnerving. At the same time, it was an opportunity for me to demonstrate an important character trait toward her—being patient, gracious, and loving. It worked. Raquel said "yes."

Courtship

The next part of the conversation was as exciting as the first. We made plans to spend time with each other throughout the week, until the day I needed to fly back to the States.

One evening we drove to the city of Ponce to hear Roy Brown and Aires Bucaneros (Buccaneer Pretensions), perform at the legendary La Perla Theater. Roy Brown had distinguished himself as a popular activist singer during the 1960s, protesting the Vietnam War, and advocating for the Island's independence from the United States. The theater was full, and the crowd enthusiastic.

On our way back to Aibonito that night, I reflected with Raquel on the meaning of the music, especially its relationship to the teachings of Jesus and the Anabaptist faith in the context of social and political realities of Puerto Rico at the time. I asked, how could Mennonites in Puerto Rico become an example of a community of faith that looked much like the early church did, caring for one another, meeting the needs of the oppressed, and practicing nonviolence? We both shared a dream of a vibrant Anabaptist Mennonite church on the Island. This dream drew our hearts closer to each other.

On another day, we stopped at El Mirador, a scenic overlook along the road from Aibonito to Cayey. We could see the entire La Plata valley where I grew up. I pointed out different locations across the valley. I told Raquel stories I experienced in those spots with my brother, family, and friends throughout my first seventeen years of life.

I told Raquel about my adventures on the *lomita*, a cone-shaped hill in the middle of the valley that looked like a miniature volcano. I had climbed it several times as a child. I showed her the visible marks of terraces that cut across the sides of the hill. On those terraces, farmers had grown sugar cane and tobacco just two or three decades before. I remembered, in particular, sugar cane growing on those terraces.

My nostalgic side drew me to memories of a small stream, often dry, that meandered along the south side of the *lomita*. From El Mirador you could not see the stream bed because it was covered by a patch of tall bamboos growing on both sides of the stream. When Richard and I were children, we loved walking to this spot with our playmates from the barrio. The bamboo stalks grew majestically into the sky. Under the stalks, thousands of fallen dry bamboo leaves carpeted the soft bed floor. On the south side of the bed, the stream had carved out over centuries a cliff that rose above us for about 20 feet. When you looked upwards, the bamboo stalks rose 30 feet up into the air. They grew on both sides of the stream bed, and then curved at the top toward each other, forming something like a large, cool room with a cathedral high ceiling. For us children, going into this carpeted room, protected by a wall, felt like going into a home. This became our natural playhouse.

On my last vacation evening, Raquel and I drove to Old San Juan where we went for dinner at La Mallorquina, a restaurant that served cuisine from Puerto Rico and Palma de Mallorca, the capital city of the Mediterranean Island of Mallorca that belonged to Spain. Don Antonio Vidal Llinás and others who opened its doors in 1848, came from Palma de

Mallorca. I ordered a traditional Mallorca paella dish, which fit well with the lovely conversation I had with Raquel. It was a lively conversation, to the point that I didn't see when the waitress removed from the table my delicious, unfinished dish. Raquel smiled, and later on in the car, laughed. She has ever since reminded me of how love-struck I was that evening.

I flew back to Pennsylvania for my second year of a two-year term as assistant director of Mennonite Central Committee's U.S. Program. I oversaw several voluntary service units in Louisiana, Minneapolis, Philadelphia, Lancaster, and Akron. I also administered the minority job training program which placed a half-dozen young people of color from Mennonite churches in New York City and Philadelphia in Mennonite businesses in the Lancaster region to learn vocational skills in construction, clerical, and printing.

Raquel was in her second year as a staff nurse at the Mennonite General Hospital in Aibonito. She lived in the nurses' residence on the hospital grounds. Her shift was 3 to 11 p.m. As a conscientious young nurse, she often finished the required shift-transition paperwork around 12:30 to 1:00 a.m. At this hour, she and I spoke with each other over the phone. Our conversations often went for an entire hour. We couldn't have been happier, listening to each other's voices.

A Bump in the Road

However, my emotional state continued to deteriorate through the fall months of 1980. I did not recognize it as clinical depression until I started seeing a counselor in early winter.

The onset of my depression had actually started two years earlier, in the fall of 1978, when I was in my senior year at Eastern Mennonite College. This happened right after an exhilarating junior year in Washington, D.C. when I participated in Eastern Mennonite College's Washington Study Service Year. Once I got back on the main campus in Harrisonburg, Virginia, I began to dread my next steps after college. However, my senior year began on a positive note. Albert Keim, the academic dean, recruited me as his student assistant. I also directed the first-ever Office of Cross Cultural Affairs. I dreamed of going to graduate school. I wanted to apply for a master's degree in sociology or urban planning. I targeted the University of Michigan. Did I apply? Was I rejected? I don't remember. All I know is that my hunger for graduate school diminished as the fall months melded into the winter months.

In the early spring of 1979, I was overjoyed when Lynn Roth hired me at the U.S. Program of Mennonite Central Committee. However, the hire did not seem to stave off my growing depression. During the spring trimester, I had difficulty completing the remaining credits for my bachelor's degree in psychology. I dropped the Abnormal Psychology course, and agreed to take it during the summer term in June and July.

In April, Al Keim allowed me to go home to Puerto Rico for four weeks, so I could concentrate on completing my course load. The time I spent at home and at the library of the University of Puerto Rico helped me focus on my studies. It protected me from distractions of over-involvement with my on-campus job.

In July, I took a three-week course entitled, "Community, Technology and Environment," with Paul Peachy, sociology professor at Catholic University of America. Paul actually taught the course on the property of the recently established Rolling Ridge Study Retreat Center near Shepherdstown, West Virginia. During these days, rays of hope shined through my clouds of sadness.

So, two years later in the summer, fall, and winter months of 1980 and early 1981, Raquel and I continued to cultivate our relationship miles away from each other. We wrote letters and made phone calls to each other. During this time, Ruth Stover, the administrator of Academia Menonita in Guaynabo, Puerto Rico, recruited me to teach Bible and serve as guidance counselor at this K-12 school, starting in the fall of 1981. Getting a job in Puerto Rico meant that Raquel and I could be close to each other.

But by the early months of 1981, my clinical depression had gotten worse. I was unable to concentrate on my day-to-day tasks. I had difficulty writing. My speech began to slur. I could not sleep well. When I did, I felt like I was falling into a dark bottomless pit. I felt utterly helpless. I did not know how to get out my depression. I was scared.

I stopped writing letters to Raquel. I was not calling her on the phone either. I felt I had nothing to say. I did not tell her about my depression. Raquel was worried. She thought I had stopped loving her, and was ready to break our relationship. However, I still kept in touch by phone with my mother. One Sunday morning after the church service at the Aibonito Mennonite Church, my mother told Raquel about my depression. Raquel then understood.

This happened around March. My counselor realized the severity of my illness. He referred me to a psychiatrist who could subscribe medication. I made an appointment. The psychiatrist gave me a prescription of anti-depressants. Within two weeks, my depression lifted completely. I took the anti-depressants for another two weeks, then stopped using them. My outlook in life changed. A whole new world opened before my eyes. I could articulate well. I could write. I thrust myself back into my loving relationship with Raquel. It was like a miracle. I never again had to take an anti-depressant. I felt hope. The obstacles of life no longer prevented me from living and loving at my fullest.

Preparation for the Big Event

When I arrived in Puerto Rico in early summer, Raquel and I started to make plans for a wedding. At first, I wanted to marry within six months. However, Raquel preferred a one-year waiting period. She prevailed.

Soon after arriving in Puerto Rico, Raquel's brother Héctor and his wife Milly invited us to their apartment in Juncos for a family gathering and meal. In keeping with Puerto Rican traditions, this was my opportunity to ask Doña Modesta,

Raquel's mother, for Raquel's hand, now that Raquel and I had become *novios*. Asking for Raquel's hand was scary. It showed my introverted side. And yet, I was grateful for the courage that sprung from my heart to speak directly to Doña Modesta, and show Raquel's mother the love I had for Raquel. It was a meaningful moment for me, Raquel, and Raquel's entire family.

We got engaged in a festive summer family celebration at the house of Ita, Raquel's sister. At the time Ita and her family lived in Palmas del Mar, just outside the city of Humacao, a beautiful location for the event. Pearl Kurtz and Martha Byers, friends from the Lancaster household where I had lived in Pennsylvania during my previous two years, also came for the engagement.

During the 1981-1982 school year at Academia Menonita, I lived at the Evangelical Seminary of Puerto Rico in Hato Rey, about 15 minutes from Summit Hills, where the school was located. Both places were within the larger San Juan metropolitan area. Raquel had started a new job in the pediatric intensive care unit of the government's Regional Hospital in Caguas. We saw each other two or three days a week throughout the year. Caguas was about 25 minutes away from Hato Rey. Being together was always a joy. We went to the movie theater together. We ate dinner together, often at Kentucky Fried Chicken, our favorite. Sometimes we drove to Certenejas of Cidra for a view of Caguas whose lights sparkled brightly in the dark night. At places like this, Raquel and I dreamed about what our lives together would be like many years into the future.

On weekends, Raquel and I attended Sunday morning services at the Aibonito Mennonite Church. On one or two occasions, worship leaders asked Raquel and me to sing a special song. We were happy to do so. We enjoyed blending our voices in harmony.

In the spring of 1982, we attended a three-day pre-marriage retreat at Casa Manresa in Aibonito. Since neither of us were raised Catholic, Raquel and I had never visited this retreat center, even though it was one of the most influential religious institutions in the central mountains of the Island. The Jesuits organized the retreat. They invited speakers who were marriage counselors, priests, and physicians. These professionals provided psychological, sociological, faith, and medical perspectives on marriage. We also heard from a panel of exemplary married couples about their experiences in creating strong marriages. We stayed in small bare rooms with a bed, a desk, and a lamp on a night stand that invited contemplation. Men stayed in one section of the building, and women in another. The Jesuits also scheduled quiet time for prayer, meditation, and journaling. With love songs playing in the hallways, we were asked to reflect on human love, and most importantly, in our loving relationship with God.

Marriage Celebration

The wedding day arrived on July 3, 1982. We asked Luis Abraham Ortiz, my cousin's brother-in-law and a notable artist in Puerto Rico, to create our wedding invitation cards. Luis Abraham, whom we knew as Bimbán, used silk screen techniques to print on the card the silhouette of a young couple holding hands. We invited friends and family, and the entire Aibonito Mennonite congregation to attend. Over 200 guests filled the church. Ushers had to place additional chairs in the foyer and the balcony. Raúl, my former pastor, and Raquel's brother-in-law, married us. We asked three ministers to give short meditations: David Powell, Enrique Ortiz, and my Uncle Don Brenneman. The Félix family, well-known in evangelical churches across the Island for their operatic voices, sang several moving songs. Esther Rose Graber accompanied them on the piano. Raquel and I read the marriage vows we had written for each other.

Everyone who attended the wedding was also welcomed to the reception on the lawn of my parent's home in La Plata. Many friends came that evening. Raquel and I hired Luis Mercado, from La Plata, as the caterer for the delicious food.

We asked a good friend and church member at the Aibonito Mennonite Church, José Luis Vázquez, to serve as our photographer. The reception was informal, not elaborate. It was simply a time when people could engage in conversation with each other, and enjoy delicious food at the same time.

We left the reception late in the evening, and drove to the house in Villa Carmen of Caguas to begin our lives together as husband and wife. We woke up early for our flight to Saint Thomas, Virgin Islands, on Sunday morning, July 4, where we started our honeymoon week—three days and two nights in St. Thomas, one night back in Puerto Rico at Parador Guajataca on the north coast of the Island, and three nights at a cabin in the Centro Vacacional del Monte del Estado, in Maricao, from which we drove daily to the Boquerón beach in Cabo Rojo during the day. It was a memorable trip to start our married life.

Our First Years Together

During our first year of marriage, we attended another Jesuit-led retreat at Casa Manresa. This time, it was a marriage encounter geared to strengthen the bonds of married couples. It was inspiring as the pre-marriage retreat had been the year before.

Raquel and I also helped organize a group of several young married couples from Aibonito Mennonite Church and from the community. We had several gatherings where we met to discuss topics of mutual interest, to support and encourage each other, and to eat together. Angie and Delmer Schlabach, Lizzie and Luis Elier Rodríguez, Titi and Federico Rosado, Nayda and Andrés Díaz, were some among several others who came to these gatherings. These friends became the community of support for Raquel and me over the next two years, before we headed north to the United States for new adventures in our married life.

Chapter 11

UNA APRECIADA TRAYECTORIA

José E. Jiménez Burgos

Hola, un saludo desde la Isla del Encanto a todos los lectores de esta colección de historias que intentan labrar un conjunto de experiencias de la vida como menonita en nuestro querido Puerto Rico.

Deseo iniciar este recorrido de mi vida expresando que me crié en el municipio de Cayey, un pueblo en el área central de la Isla a 40 minutos de la capital, San Juan. La crianza se desarrolló en un hogar un tanto disfuncional con un padre alcohólico, y una madre dedicada completamente a los quehaceres del hogar. Ambos con baja escolaridad, pues ninguno pudo llegar a la secundaria por la escasez económica en sus años de infancia. Somos seis hermanos, tres varones y tres hembras, y yo soy el menor de todos.

Mis Inicios Religiosos

A pesar de que no teníamos educación religiosa formal, nuestros padres no impedían que asistiéramos a la iglesia de nuestra preferencia. Fue así que di mis primeros pasos en la iglesia católica, cuando una las catequistas de la comunidad le pidió a mi madre que me permitiera tomar la catequesis para hacer la primera comunión. Éste fue mi primer paso en el mundo religioso a la edad de unos ocho años.

Luego de mi inicio con la Iglesia Católica, tuve contacto con la Iglesia Bautista de mi pueblo de Cayey cuando tenía unos once o doce años. Ésta fue una experiencia muy interesante. Un líder de la iglesia, llamado Natanael, buscaba adolescentes en las casas todos los sábados y, con la autorización de los padres, nos llevaba al parque de pelota del barrio La Plata en Aibonito. Una vez allí, nos dirigía en un momento de oración y un devocional corto para luego dividirnos en dos equipos y pasar la mañana jugando softball. Al concluir el partido pasábamos a una casa donde nos esperaba un suculento almuerzo para luego regresarnos a nuestros hogares.

Al día siguiente, el domingo, nos esperaba en el servicio de la mañana. Fue una experiencia que ahora como adulto y pastor valoro mucho. Creo que fueron mis primeros pasos en el conocimiento del cristianismo de manera auténtica, y el inicio de una relación con Dios que ha durado hasta el día de hoy.

Mi Encuentro con los Menonitas

Al cabo de varios años después, en la década del 1970, la Iglesia Menonita Betzaida, en el barrio Honduras del municipio de Cidra, que pastoreaba el hermano Miguel A. Rolón, comenzó una obra en el barrio Mogote del municipio de Cayey. Ahí vivía mi familia. El impacto de los hermanos menonitas en nuestra localidad fue extraordinario. Visitaban hogares y celebraban cultos, campañas evangelísticas y actividades con los jóvenes de la comunidad.

Así poco a poco los menonitas fueron ganando terreno en el barrio hasta que un día mi hermano mayor, Rafael, quien padecía de epilepsia y retraso mental, fue impactado por la predicación de los menonitas y pidió que celebraran un servicio en nuestro hogar. Esa noche, mi madre, mi hermano Rafael, mi hermana Carmen y su esposo Roger, hicieron profesión de fe y comenzaron un peregrinar hacia la iglesia menonita, el cual aún persiste en la mayoría de ellos. Digo que aún persiste porque mi madre partió con el Señor y mi hermana y su esposo ahora perseveran en la Iglesia Menonita del barrio La Plata. Mi hermano Rafael, mientras tanto, está al cuidado de otra hermana nuestra, Eva, y por razones de salud no puede asistir a la iglesia.

En el 1975 hice profesión de fe en la Iglesia Menonita del barrio Honduras. Comencé asistiendo a la obra que esta iglesia estaba levantando en el barrio Mogote, como mencioné anteriormente. Nos reuníamos allí todos los miércoles para tener un momento de oración y estudio bíblico. Fueron unos años maravillosos de crecimiento espiritual y de conocimiento de la Palabra de Dios. A la edad de 15 años fui a las aguas bautismales abrazando así oficialmente la fe menonita.

Involucrándome en la Iglesia

Los hermanos que formábamos la obra de Mogote participábamos de las actividades de la iglesia madre que estaba ubicada en el barrio Honduras. Allí comencé a involucrarme en actividades con los jóvenes de la iglesia y a relacionarme más con éstos creando una amistad muy cercana con muchos de ellos. Compartíamos en la escuela pública, en actividades familiares y, por supuesto, en todas las actividades de la congregación.

A los pocos años de participar de la iglesia me permitieron ser el chofer de la guagua que transportaba a los hermanos y a las hermanas desde la obra en Mogote hasta el templo en el barrio Honduras. Para las actividades y el servicio de nuestra iglesia yo pasaba a recogerlos a sus hogares, participábamos del servicio y luego los llevaba a sus casas. Fueron unos años maravillosos en los que compartí y disfruté en estos viajes con los hermanos.

Poco a poco fui teniendo oportunidades en la congregación. El pastor, Miguel A. Rolón, me fue dando oportunidades de servicio en diferentes áreas que me permitieron crecer rápidamente. Junto a él y a otro hermano participamos por varios años de un programa radial que se transmitía todos los domingos a las siete de la mañana, "La Hora de la Reformación". El programa duraba 30 minutos y tenía una variedad de música cristiana, reflexión y la proclamación de la Palabra de Dios. También participé del diaconado, como maestro de escuela dominical y de escuela bíblica de verano, además de dar mis primeros pasos en la predicación. Éste fue un tiempo de constante aprendizaje.

En muchas ocasiones me involucré en discusiones que reflexionando ahora me parecen estériles, pero que en aquel entonces eran importantes para mí. Discutí con mi primera catequista católica, con algunos maestros de la escuela pública, en fin vivía una experiencia donde creía y quería que todos pensaran y creyeran como yo.

Ampliando mis Horizontes en la Denominación

A los pocos años de estar participando de las actividades de la congregación me dieron la oportunidad de formar parte de la directiva de la Juventud Evangélica Menonita Puertorriqueña (JEMP). Esto fue algo muy gratificante, ya que me permitía relacionarme con jóvenes y líderes de todas las congregaciones menonitas de Puerto Rico. Se ampliaba mi visión de iglesia, del liderato y de la inclusión. Aprendí que había más gente, más hermanos, más líderes y más maneras de vivir la vida cristiana además de la que estaba viviendo en mi iglesia local. La JEMP me proyectó hacia la denominación.

Un tiempo después de colaborar en la JEMP me llegó la oportunidad de formar parte del Concilio de las Iglesias Menonitas de Puerto Rico. Por varios años participé del Concilio en una experiencia de trabajo que amplió mi perspectiva de iglesia al tener que trabajar con todos los asuntos que forman parte de la denominación: iglesias, instituciones y organizaciones. Fue una verdadera escuela para mí.

Durante esta época me relacioné con pastores y líderes de las iglesias menonitas dentro y fuera de Puerto Rico. Conocí pastores de Estados Unidos y Centro y Sur América con quienes desarrollé una bonita amistad y una buena relación. De ellos fui aprendiendo el valor y el sacrificio del ministerio pastoral.

Recuerdo con mucha satisfacción los momentos vividos con varios de ellos, pero en especial con los de mi pastor Miguel A. Rolón. Él fue mi maestro, mi mentor y un ejemplo de una pastoral de entrega, con un alto sentido de la ética ministerial y de la responsabilidad con la iglesia y la denominación. También recuerdo a Elier Rodríguez y su convicción de una importancia de la educación teológica en los líderes de nuestra iglesia y su aportación a la educación de la comunidad de fe.

Nuevas Empresas

A los 21 años de edad contraje matrimonio con Vilma Rolón, hija de mi pastor Miguel A. Rolón. Iniciamos bien jóvenes, pues ella tenia sólo 20 años, un maravilloso viaje por la vida matrimonial y ministerial.

A los diez meses de estar casados comenzamos nuestra primera experiencia pastoral en la iglesia menonita del pueblo de Coamo. Esta iglesia nos abrió sus puertas y su corazón. Para ser mi primera experiencia pastoral fue algo maravilloso. Vilma y yo tenemos recuerdos muy bonitos de los hermanos y las hermanas de esta congregación. Vilma siempre comenta que no quería casarse con un pastor, porque era hija de pastor, y sabía lo que representaba ser esposa de uno. No obstante la experiencia fue muy linda para ambos.

Estando trabajando ahí nacieron nuestros hijos Keren, Kamyl y Kelvin. Los hermanos de la iglesia se portaron de forma increíble con su ayuda en el proceso de crianza de nuestros hijos.

En esta comunidad de fe trabajamos por alrededor de ocho años hasta que pasé a laborar como Secretario Ejecutivo de la denominación. Éste fue un ministerio breve, pues sólo duró dos años. Estuvo lleno de retos, desafíos y experiencias buenas y malas. Estando en la oficina de la Convención tuve la oportunidad de viajar a Centro y Sur América, así como a los Estados Unidos. Participé de varias Consultas de la Iglesia Menonita Latinoamericana en Guatemala, Uruguay, en encuentros como CAMCA en Honduras, y varios talleres con el Seminario Semilla.

Enfrentando Retos

Estando en el ministerio de la Secretaría Ejecutiva, viví la triste experiencia de que varias de las iglesias de la denominación tomaron la decisión de abandonar la Convención Menonita. Una que me afectó mucho fue la iglesia donde nací y crecí con la iglesia menonita, la del barrio Honduras. Ya mi suegro no pastoreaba allí; él estaba desarrollando su ministerio en la ciudad de Ponce. Entonces el pastor que estaba dirigiendo la iglesia convenció a la congregación para que se desafiliara de la denominación. Fue como un contagio, ya que detrás de ésta se desasociaran las iglesias menonitas de Arecibo y de Hatillo.

Tanto el Concilio como yo hicimos lo indecible por evitar que esto no ocurriera, pero razones doctrinales pesaron más en la decisión, y las iglesias terminaron desafiliándose. Ésta ha sido una de las experiencias más difíciles para mí. No podía aceptar que como hermanos en la fe no pudiéramos superar las diferencias y llegar al extremo de romper nuestras afiliaciones.

Después de varios esfuerzos estas iglesias continuaron su ministerio separadas de nuestra denominación. Sin embargo, en el momento mantenemos una relación de amistad y de compañerismo cristiano que nada lo ha podido romper.

Se Abren Otras Puertas

La separación de estas iglesias frustró mi deseo de seguir trabajando en la oficina como Secretario Ejecutivo. A los dos años, de un nombramiento de tres, decidí renunciar. Después de estar un año fuera del ministerio me di cuenta de que Dios me había llamado para trabajar en su obra y no en ningún trabajo secular. Así que me puse en contacto con la oficina de la denominación para poner a su disposición mis servicios pastorales.

En el 1992 fui enviado a pastorear la Iglesia Menonita de Cayey. Éste fue un puesto interino. Duró dos años intensos, de buenos resultados, sin embargo no era allí donde me quería Dios. El Señor me fue preparando y llevando a colaborar con su reino desde el Hospital Menonita de Aibonito.

En el 1994 comencé a laborar como capellán del programa de Hospicio del Hospital Menonita. Fue en este ministerio que Dios me llevó a comprender la importancia del acompañamiento en el proceso de duelo de la gente. Fue una experiencia de mucho crecimiento para mí al encontrarme con las personas en su proceso de transición a la otra vida. En un ambiente totalmente ecuménico, el programa ofrece apoyo al paciente y a la familia desde su fe y sus creencias en la preparación para la muerte. Es una verdadera escuela de teología tanatológica.

Estando de capellán en este programa tomé una unidad de Clinical Pastoral Education. Durante el tiempo que estudié estos cursos pude comprender la importancia de la educación teológica en aquellos que aspiramos a servir desde el ministerio a Dios.

Tomando las clases descubrí también que mi proceso de formación estaba trunco y afectado por la crianza de un hogar disfuncional. Algo que aprendí fue que una de las características de hijos adultos de padres alcohólicos es que generalmente no terminan la mayoría de los proyectos que emprenden. Una de las cosas inconclusas en mi vida era mi formación educativa. En varias ocasiones había intentado terminar mis estudios universitarios, y por algunas "razones" no los había podido concluir. En el proceso de tomar la unidad de Clinical Pastoral Education descubrí esa realidad en mi vida, y me hice el propósito de romper de alguna manera con esa característica. De tal forma fui a solicitar admisión al Seminario Evangélico de Puerto Rico.

Luego de un proceso de orientación fui admitido al Seminario. Me mantuve estudiando, mientras trabajaba por espacio de cuatro años, hasta que logré adquirir mi título de Maestría en Artes en Religión. Fue una experiencia maravillosa para mí. Me ha ayudado en mi ministerio pastoral y me ha permitido emprender el camino para romper con aquellas conductas típicas y características de un hogar disfuncional. El Seminario me brindó unas herramientas excelentes para poder continuar mi desarrollo como capellán del Hospital Menonita tanto como de pastor de una iglesia. Igualmente la maestría me abrió las puertas para enseñar en la Universidad Interamericana de Puerto Rico los cursos de Fe Cristiana y Filosofía desde una perspectiva humanística.

Un Nuevo Pastorado

Compartía mi tiempo entre la Universidad y la Capellanía del Hospital cuando la Iglesia Menonita de Aibonito me llamó para que fuera su pastor. Era un reto grande para mí, toda vez que la iglesia de Aibonito es una de las más grandes de la denominación y recién había terminado de ser pastoreada por Enrique Ortiz. Ortiz era un pastor de mucha experiencia en nuestra denominación y tenía muchos años de servicio a esta iglesia. Luego de orar al Señor y de consultarlo con mi esposa y mi familia, acepté el reto de pastorear la Iglesia de Aibonito. Concluí mi función como profesor de la Universidad Interamericana, y dividí mi tiempo entre la capellanía del Hospital de Aibonito y la pastoral de la iglesia menonita en dicho pueblo.

La experiencia como pastor de la iglesia Menonita de Aibonito ha sido extraordinaria. Con esta iglesia mi familia y yo hemos aprendido el valor de la comprensión, la tolerancia, la misericordia, la bondad y la hospitalidad. Todas estas manifestaciones de los atributos de Dios, esta congregación los ha demostrado con mi familia y conmigo. De la misma manera lo ha hecho con todas las personas que llegan a nuestra comunidad de fe. Hemos pasado momentos muy difíciles en nuestro hogar y siempre hemos tenido el apoyo y el respaldo incondicionales de estos hermanos como nunca lo imaginé.

Hemos crecido juntos en una experiencia de conocimiento, adoración y servicio a Dios. Experimentamos las vivencias del reino de Dios y su amor en todas las reuniones y en todos los servicios que celebramos. Gracias doy a Dios por esta congregación. Ya llevamos 13 años sirviendo a los hermanos de este lugar y nos sentimos como si hubiéramos comenzado ayer.

Todas las reuniones son una experiencia nueva y reconfortante para ellos y para mi familia.

En el presente comparto el ministerio de la iglesia con la dirección del Programa de Apoyo Pastoral y Servicios de Capellanía del Sistema de Salud Menonita. Es un programa que lleva dos años de estar implementándose e incluye a capellanes en los hospitales de Caguas, Cayey y Aibonito. Como director trabajo, junto con los demás capellanes, en la implementación de planes y de proyectos para mejorar la calidad de servicio espiritual que ofrecemos a nuestros pacientes, familiares y compañeros de trabajo.

Reflexiones

Han pasado cuarenta y un años desde que conocí a mi Señor, y todavía le sirvo. Hace treinta y cuatro años que soy ministro ordenado de la Convención de Iglesias Menonitas de Puerto Rico, y casi treinta y cinco de estar casado con Vilma. No me arrepiento de ninguna de estas tres grandes decisiones que he tomado en la vida. Las mismas se entrelazan, y pienso que hubiera sido muy difícil si faltara alguna de ellas. La iglesia menonita, el ministerio, y mi esposa, han llenado mi vida por los pasados 41 años. Por todo esto le agradezco a Dios, y por permitirme una valorada vivencia menonita en Puerto Rico.

Muchas gracias por la oportunidad de compartir mi experiencia con ustedes.

Dios les bendiga.

Chapter 12

ELLOS HICIERON LA DIFERENCIA

Nilsa Pagán Rosado

"Los que sembraron con lágrimas, con regocijo segarán. Irá andando y llorando el que lleva la preciosa semilla; mas volverá a venir con regocijo, trayendo sus gavillas".
Salmo 126: 5-6

Doy gracias a Dios porque un día los misioneros menonitas sembraron en Puerto Rico, la Isla del Encanto, la preciosa semilla de la palabra de Dios. Andando por campo y pueblo, con lluvia o sol, caminando o en carro, fueron sembrando la preciosa semilla. Mi familia y yo somos fruto de esa semilla preciosa que sembraron estos misioneros en el pueblo de Aibonito.

Nací un 16 de octubre de 1957 en el Hospital General Menonita del pueblo de Aibonito. Mis padres fueron el señor Rafael Pagán Collazo y la señora Paula Rosado Alicea, oriundos también de Aibonito. Soy la segunda de seis hermanos. Todos nacimos y nos criamos en Aibonito: María Migdalia, Carmen L. (Cita), Rafael (Papo), Paula Ivette (Poly), Elaury y yo.

Mi Introducción a los Menonitas

En el año 1963 mi padre se afilió a la Iglesia Evangélica Menonita de Aibonito, aceptando al Señor como su Salvador.

Aunque mi tía Juanita Rosado Alicea y mis primos Maruchi, Rosin, Fernando y Federico, ya asistían a la iglesia y le servían al Señor, fue a través de mi padre que llegamos a la Iglesia Menonita.

¡Qué mucho disfrutábamos de ese tiempo en la Iglesia Menonita! Recuerdo con mucho cariño que durante los años de mi niñez la iglesia ofrecía una escuelita bíblica de verano en la cual daban historias de la Biblia, juegos, y ricas meriendas. De mis años de juventud vienen a mi memoria grandes eventos como el campamento de verano de jóvenes, los dramas de Navidad, las cantatas de Resurrección y de Navidad, y tantos otros.

De todos estos eventos, era el campamento de verano el que más me disfrutaba. En éste teníamos la oportunidad de conocer y hacer amistad con jóvenes de las otras iglesias. Este campamento se llevaba a cabo en el pueblo de Juana Díaz. Muchos son los buenos recuerdos, tanto de lo que nos alimentábamos espiritualmente, como también de las travesuras y los deportes que ejercíamos. La última noche era la que se llevaba a cabo la famosa fogata. Cantábamos coritos, se asaban *hot dogs* y también *marshmallows*. Había momentos de reflexión muy especiales. ¡Qué bien lo pasábamos! Y las serenatas, ¡cómo las gozábamos! Tiempos que no volverán.

Personas Claves en mi Desarrollo

Mi padre falleció en 1965. Los hermanos John y Bonita Driver, pastores de la Iglesia Menonita de Aibonito en esa época, nos dieron una demostración de amor cristiano que ha tenido un peso sinigual en mi vida. Estos hermanos, con la asistencia de Dios, ayudaron a recuperarnos de nuestra terrible pérdida. Mi madre había quedado viuda, totalmente devastada, y con cuatro niños, y uno en su vientre.

Con los Driver comenzamos a tener muchas experiencias inolvidables. Recuerdo con mucho cariño que ellos, por un tiempo, nos llevaban a su casa todos los fines de semana y nos enseñaban acerca de Dios, y también a hacer cosas del hogar.

Fue ahí que obtuve mis primeras experiencias horneando ricas galletitas, bizcochos y otra repostería.

Otras personas de gran bendición a mi vida lo fueron las muy queridas y recordadas Carol Glick, Ana K. Massanari y Mary Ellen Yoder. Estas tres mujeres, además de ser grandes siervas del Señor, fueron parte de mi familia. Junto a ellas pasé las mejores Navidades de mi vida. Siempre nos reuníamos en su casa en la Nochebuena. Mis hermanos, primos y yo disfrutábamos tanto ese tiempo. Jugábamos "ping pong" y nos divertíamos mucho con los juegos de mesa. También cantábamos villancicos de Navidad frente al hermoso árbol que éstas decoraban. Compartíamos los deliciosos platos de nuestra tradicional cena de Navidad: arroz con gandules, pasteles, pernil y los ricos postres típicos de la época. Pero lo mejor era esperar hasta la medianoche cuando nos repartían los tan esperados regalos de Navidad. ¡Cuánto disfrutaba junto a mis hermanos y el resto de la familia de esta hermosa fiesta de Navidad, recordando que el nacimiento del Niño Jesús era el verdadero significado de la temporada; algo que ellas nos enseñaron a recordar y celebrar.

Mis Maestros en Betania

En el año 1966 llegamos a la Academia Menonita Betania. Yo cursaba el cuarto grado, mi hermana mayor el quinto, mi otra hermana el tercero y mi hermano el primero. Durante este tiempo en la escuela fueron muchas las experiencias y las enseñanzas que adquirimos. Primero, tuvimos el privilegio de estudiar en una escuela con principios cristianos. Después, tuvimos el honor de aprender bien el idioma inglés, porque muchos de los maestros eran estadounidenses que no hablaban mucho español. De esta forma fuimos aprendiendo el idioma y disfrutamos de una calidad de enseñanza con múltiples valores.

En Betania y en la iglesia conocimos y tuvimos el privilegio de interactuar con muchos obreros de la Iglesia Menonita. Éstos calaron profundamente en mi familia. No podría mencionarlos a todos, pero siempre recuerdo con mucho cariño a Carolyn

Amstutz. Ella era maestra de inglés y se hizo muy amiga de mi mamá. Carolyn nos llevó por primera vez a uno de los lugares más bellos y concurridos en Puerto Rico: las Cabañas de Boquerón en Cabo Rojo. Fue uno de los primeros viajes que tuvimos después de la muerte de mi padre. Recuerdo que fuimos en una guagua Volkswagen que usaban en la casa de los voluntarios que venían a trabajar en la escuela, el hospital y la iglesia. Fue una experiencia que siempre atesoraré en mi corazón.

Otra maestra que también formó parte bien importante en mi familia fue la señora Rose Fuentes. Fue maestra de mi querido hermano Papo en primer grado. Su hija mayor fue mi mejor amiga en la escuela, y con ella aprendí a correr bicicleta. Rose Fuentes fue otra de las grandes amigas y compañeras de trabajo que tuvo mi mamá mientras trabajaba en Betania. Ellas compartieron muchos momentos que hasta el día de hoy llevamos muy presentes en el corazón.

Carolyn Holderread fue mi muy recordada y querida maestra de inglés desde sexto a séptimo grados. Recuerdo muy bien lo mucho que aprendí con ella para tener una buena pronunciación en el inglés. Era mi maestra favorita, y la admiraba tanto que quería copiar todos sus gestos y por eso trataba de pronunciar tal y como ella hablaba el inglés.

Fue en en el octavo grado de la Academia Betania que tomé la decisión más importante de mi vida. Acepté al Señor como mi Salvador personal con Alicia Kehl, mi maestra de Biblia.

Alicia era una misionera canadiense que luchó incansablemente por la ganancia de almas. Muchas veces llegó a la casa de mi tía Guanes caminando porque venía de evangelizar en algún lugar cercano. A la hora que llegara a nuestra casa siempre era bien recibida. Ella era un vivo ejemplo de Jesús cuando caminaba con sus discípulos predicando y sanando a la gente. Aunque no sanó a ningún enfermo, sí cumplió con la gran comisión de "ir y predicar el evangelio a toda criatura". A través de ella muchos llegaron a conocer y a aceptar a Jesús como el Salvador de sus vidas, y entre esas personas me incluyo yo. ¡Qué gran bendición! Una de las cosas que la caracterizaba eran los coritos que dirigía con tanto ánimo. Nunca olvidaré ese tiempo viviendo junto a esta gran misionera. Alicia fue un gran ejemplo a seguir.

Los Directores y la Música en Betania

Así como maestros que dejaron huellas, hubo también directores de la escuela que hicieron una gran labor misionera. Entre éstos puedo mencionar al señor Merle Sommers. Éste, además de haber sido director, fungió como maestro de música y director del coro de la escuela. Fue en el coro de Betania donde desarrollé el talento de cantar que Dios había puesto en mí. Durante estos años escolares siempre pertenecí al coro, algo que disfrutaba muchísimo. Esta actividad musical era una gran pasión para mí.

También Carol Glick, que fue principal de la escuela por muchísimos años, fungió como directora del coro. Una de las actividades del coro que más disfruté fue la rondalla de Navidad que dirigió ella. Fuimos por diferentes comunidades y lugares en el pueblo de Aibonito llevando los villancicos de Navidad o las parrandas navideñas. Uno de los villancicos que más recuerdo era el de *Go tell it on the mountain*. Fue una de las más hermosas y gratificantes experiencias que viví en mis años de vida en Betania.

Hubo otros directores que recuerdo y que fueron de gran ayuda para el desarrollo y el funcionamiento de la Academia Menonita Betania. Entre ellos están los boricuas María H. Rosado (mejor conocida como Maruchi), Ángel Rafael Falcón y María H. Díaz.

Actividades Recreativas en Betania

Algo que no puedo dejar de mencionar de mis memorias de la Academia Menonita Betania fue el famoso juego de "la bola de puño". Todo aquel que pasó por Betania hasta el año 1994, más o menos, tiene que saber lo que era jugar "la bola de puño". Era una bola con una soga atada a un tubo, el cual estaba cimentado en una plataforma redonda de cemento dividida en dos partes. El juego consistía en tratar de enrollar completamente la soga con la bola en el tubo. Esto, claro, si el jugador del lado contrario te lo permitía. Había que hacer largas filas para poder participar de la actividad en la hora de recreo. ¡Cúan divertido y ejercitado era ese juego! ¡Qué tiempos tan gratos!

También teníamos la cancha donde se jugaba baloncesto y volibol, mi deporte preferido. A parte de eso teníamos un parque donde se jugaba *softball*, el cual no era de mucho agrado para mí. Pertenecí al equipo de volibol femenino y fuimos por varias ocasiones a competir con otras escuelas del pueblo y a otros pueblos adyacentes a Aibonito. La clase de educación física no era una de mis favoritas, pero recuerdo siempre con mucho cariño a uno de mis maestros de esa clase, Mr. Larry Yoder, quien era miembro del Servicio Voluntario Menonita.

Otros Apreciados Obreros Menonitas Norteamericanos

Fueron muchos los obreros menonitas norteamericanos que pasaron por la Isla dejando sus huellas muy marcadas y bien recordadas. Muchos sirvieron en la Iglesia Menonita isleña como líderes y pastores junto a sus esposas e hijos. Recuerdo a Lorenzo Greaser. Lorenzo fue pastor en varias congregaciones y trabajó también de administrador en el Hospital General Menonita. Otro fue Addona Nissley. Addona sirvió como pastor en congregaciones como La Plata y Coamo. Éste tenía tres hijos y el menor, Tim, estaba en el mismo grado que yo en Betania.

Entre las muchas personas que trabajaron para el Hospital Menonita recuerdo a Royal y Florence Hower. Él era anestesiólogo y ella enfermera. También recuerdo al doctor Darrel Diener y a su esposa Leona, que era técnica de laboratorio. Además trabajó el doctor Ronald Graber, un reconocido cirujano.

Otro que viene a mi mente es David Helmuth y su familia. David sirvió como director del Instituto Bíblico Menonita, una institución que le dio grandes beneficios a muchos de los líderes de la Iglesia Menonita. Hay otras muchas personas que no recuerdo que también estuvieron rindiendo una excelente y sobresaliente labor misionera en mi amada isla de Puerto Rico, y especialmente en mi pueblo de Aibonito. Me siento muy bendecida por haber tenido a todas estas personas que de una manera u otra bendijeron mi niñez, mi adolescencia y mi juventud.

Pensamientos Finales

Bueno, pero el tiempo pasó. Crecí y me desarrollé en un ambiente cristiano. Vivo agradecida de mi Dios y de toda la enseñanza que recibí a través de estos primeros obreros y de los que vinieron después. Estoy súper agradecida de mis padres, especialmente de mi madre, que en la manera en que pudieron, nos inculcaron valores, y nos enseñaron a amar a Dios por sobre todas las cosas. Doy más que gracias a Dios porque tuve la oportunidad de tener a mi hija en la Academia Menonita Betania desde kindergarten hasta el noveno grado, y estoy gozosa porque también mi nieta pudo estudiar allí. ¡Qué bendición!

Le doy gracias a Dios por su infinita misericordia. También agradezco a todos estos hermanos menonitas que hicieron la diferencia en el desarrollo de mi vida espiritual. Doy gracias además porque éstos obedecieron y pusieron en práctica La Gran Comisión de "Id por todo el mundo y predicad el Evangelio a toda criatura" (Marcos 16:15).

EPILOGUE: A TAILPIECE

Galen Greaser

The crispy tail was my favorite part of a *lechón asao*, every crunchy bite forecasting a time when I would be asked to write the epilogue or tailpiece for these stories of growing up Mennonite in Puerto Rico. In Mexico, Mennonite is invariably associated with cheese. Mennonites and pigs' tails, on the other hand, did not elicit a comparable response anywhere as far as I knew. Still, I wondered if some unexplored Mennonite predisposition might account for my fondness for this appendix. I had my answer in a Google flash. "No Mennonite picnic is complete without barbecued pig tails..." was the comment attached to a recipe for the delicacy on familyoven.com. Next came this gem about pigs' tails on the "Cooking Dangerously" blog by Ann Allchin: "Mennonites like to eat them for some reason. Funny how those super-religious people seem to go whole hog on pork. Now that I think about it, Christians in general don't seem to have an issue with it. I guess Jesus must have given it the OK." Really? Who knew? As it turns out, lots of people like pigs' tails, besides some Mennonites, so let's just leave it at that.

A Mid-Twentieth Century Perspective

Google was not part of the experiences related in this book. Most of its contributors are of mid-twentieth century vintage. The big deal for us was the transistor. If we were lucky to save a few dollars and already had a serviceable baseball, even one wrapped in electrical tape, we could buy a portable transistor radio and walk out of the store snapping our fingers to Monna Bell's "La vida es una tombola, tom, tom, tombola,"— something we couldn't do at home, where popular music was one of the no-no's. We also heard *música popular* at the barbershop, after Dad quit cutting our hair. We would climb into the chair to the pulse of Cortijo y su Combo ("Si yo llego a saber que Perico era sordo, yo paro el tren..."), the harmonies of the Trío Vegabajeño, or the crooning of Marco Antonio Muñiz.

At home, on the other hand, we listened to the Chuck Wagon Gang or the Carter Family on WIVV, 1370 on your AM dial, the Christian radio station broadcasting from Vieques. We also wore out the grooves of "The Blackwood Brothers...on Tour," an album by the legendary southern Gospel quartet that Dad brought home from San Juan one day, along with some candy corn. We never could sing as low as J.D. Sumner and still can't, although we keep trying when we get together and replay the record "for old times' sake."

We Are Ourselves and Our Circumstances

"Yo soy yo y mi circunstancia" ("I am myself and my circumstance") is the oft-repeated phrase coined by Spanish philosopher José Ortega y Gasset to convey the idea that the encounter of our innate traits with the environment in which we chance to be immersed (historical time and place, social institutions, cultural beliefs, ways of life, family) shapes and conditions our life. "Growing up" is what we call the phase of biological and psychological maturation that finally deposits us into adulthood. It happens to everyone, except perhaps to certain presidential candidates. Growing up Mennonite in Puerto Rico, on the other hand, does not happen to everyone, although our world could be a better place if more people had or did.

The accounts in this book do recall the coming of age of young people who shared the circumstances of living in the mountains of central Puerto Rico in the latter half of the twentieth century and who were exposed at home, in school, and at church to the teachings and practices common to the Mennonite faith. Each account gives testimony to what the distinct circumstances and scope of experiences contributed to the writer's formative years. We didn't have access to great institutions of art and culture, but New Yorkers didn't have tropical jungles or the coquí. They had subways; we had *públicos*. Young people in other circumstances were exposed to racism and xenophobia, while we were taught inclusion and compassion, although in all honesty we didn't hear the term ecumenical or ecumenism until later. We had Catholic friends, but we were convinced they were wrong. In short, we became what we are, in part, because we were where we were.

Our ability to think impels us to make sense of our experiences. We build a narrative that serves to explain the why and how of what we believe ourselves to be. The process of assembling our life story is a creative act. From all the events of our lives, from what we have done, experienced and felt, we string and glue together the parts that serve to give meaning to our existence. Each life story is unique, selective, and can have several versions, one we tell ourselves and one we share with others.

Adults Within our Mennonite Orbit

The stories shared here have some common threads. The importance of the adults in our lives is one. Growing up we were still not autonomous; we were still within the circle of the significant adults in our lives. They decided matters for us—often more than we would like—provided for us, set an example, instructed, encouraged, nurtured and prepared us for the adventure. Nearly every account here includes a word of gratitude and recognition for the adults in our insular world, notably for our parents. Some of the writers were born into the Mennonite tradition. From the cradle their experience was one of assimilation and continuity. For others the road to a

Mennonite upbringing went through parents who took the bold, difficult decision of breaking with their own tradition and taking an uncharted path. The experience of these families was one of rupture and adaptation.

Once within the Mennonite orbit, whatever the path, the narrators of these accounts found adults that made an impression and a difference. Many were women and teachers. Others were just flat out good people. Who can forget Don Aurelio Bonilla, who was always eager to give his *testimonio* and finish with an emphatic a cappella condemnation of vice in all its forms:

> *No fumaremos tabaco, no, no, no;*
> *no fumaremos tabaco, no, no, no;*
> *no fumaremos tabaco porque el diablo lo fundó;*
> *no fumaremos tabaco, no, no, no.*

The song had other verses about alcohol and chewing tobacco, that I recall, and new vices have been added since his day. That simple tune stuck with us longer than any sermon we might have heard on the subject, although I retain a blurry recollection of a black-and-white movie projection shown in church on a Sunday evening about the perils of drink.

We're talking about a time when Sunday evening church was the norm and movie projections weren't, at least for us. Movie theaters were a no-go zone, along with dance halls, the inside of the Catholic church, and pool halls. There was some doubt about the appropriateness of television, and for years we didn't have one at home, so we'd sneak off to the nearest neighbor to watch the weekly episode of *"Perdidos en el espacio"* ("Lost in Space") or *lucha libre*. We always rooted for the tag team of Antonino Rocca and Puerto Rican Miguel Pérez. They were the champs. Come to think of it, considering what's shown on much of TV these days, maybe Don Aurelio should have added it to his list.

Still on the subject of the adults in our young lives, I'm glad to see that several of the contributors mentioned Doña Venancia Martínez. In addition to the *pegao* we blessed her for handing around in the Betania *comedor* after the many forgettable school lunches, Doña Venancia had helped Mom in our home when we were little kids, so we had an early, special bond with this kind, cheerful, and beloved Christian lady. Even Pastor Jiménez, who came into the church as a teenager by his own choice and did not grow up in a Mennonite household, acknowledges the contribution to his Christian growth by the adults in his circle of faith.

Rural Adventures (and Misadventures)

Many of the anecdotes found here happened in rural areas, another thread that runs through these accounts. Even for those of us who eventually moved to town, the countryside was always near at hand. The stories included in this book span from the mid-1940's (Dr. Weldon Troyer) to one that is nearly current (Pastor José E. Jiménez), from the open-sided tabernacle in Pulguillas to the work carried on in the congregations now. A Mennonite presence today can be found in important urban centers, but it started as rural service in the community of La Plata, before expanding to other rural areas such as Pulguillas, Palo Hincado, Coamo Arriba, and Rabanal. The focus of the Ulrich Foundation mentioned by some of the writers was also on agricultural issues related to soil conservation, animal husbandry, and pasture improvement.

As many of the stories here are about experiences in the early decades of the Mennonites in Puerto Rico, they feature rural events. The adventures and misadventures with farm animals related by several contributors are entertaining and even harrowing. Carolyn Holderread's guinea hen massacre and Rafo Falcon's losing tug-of-war with Facundo, the goat, are classic. Several articles refer to loose cattle on merry romps, and the reliance on horses to access difficult sites. And of course you can't have stories about growing up without a few spills and tumbles, although not everyone picks a silo or a water drum for the experience. Through the big side openings of the classrooms at Betania School we could often hear the mules braying and see them kicking at each other in the adjoining pasture, and we knew it was noon when we heard the shrill whistle from Don Antonio Emanuelli's coffee processing hacienda on the opposite side of the ravine.

Just getting to school meant for some of us a ride through the countryside in *la camioneta*, the improvised school bus with wooden benches for seats and the sliding ladder that pinched the fingers of more than one careless ladder operator. You might have been half asleep when you placed your skinny behind on one of those wooden planks, but it didn't take long to be bounced awake, ready to take a turn on the tetherball if time allowed when you reached the school's playground. The legendary *camioneta* still rolls over those country roads in the memories of its many riders.

Church and School as Part of our Lives

As we would expect, church life and school life are a recurring subject for the writers in this book. Many mention Summer Bible School, youth camps, and Christmas caroling as memorable events, but the accounts also suggest the assimilation and application of Mennonite teachings in the daily life of the writers. The references to conscientious objectors and I-W workers points to the Mennonite emphasis on compassionate peacemaking. The sense of being different and being perceived as such noted by several of the authors denotes the notion we were taught of being in the world but separate from it. The belief that the body is the temple of God found its practical application in the injunction against addictive substances and the temptations of the flesh prompted by activities such as dancing. Popular music and movies were considered hostile to spiritual development. The examples of service and sharing they observed in their elders made an impression on these young minds.

Schooling at Betania left its own set of impressions. Most of us had a favorite teacher or two and several garner repeated references in these accounts: Carol Glick, Anna Kay Massanari,

Rose Fuentes, Patricia Brenneman, and others. I could add Mercedes Meléndez, who I believe wrote the words for the school song: "*Amo a mi escuela Betania por su enseñar, por su ambiente saludable que me inspira cada instante luchando a triunfar...*". I think Merle Sommers, our music teacher, added the music, but I could be wrong.

I'm not wrong, however, about the lasting persistence of the tunes we learned in his music classes. From out of nowhere I might still surprise myself singing "*Alouette, gentille alouette, Alouette je te plumerai...*". We didn't know it was French and about plucking the feathers from a lark, but it stuck, as did "*Mambrú se fue a la Guerra, que dolor que dolor que pena...*", and other merry tunes. Added to these are the many *coritos* we learned ("*Yo quiero más y más de Cristo...*", "*Del vivo pan he de comer...*"), etc.

We sang one song so often it's permanently stamped in our DNA. Every day before lunch we sang "*Padre benigno*" while we stood in line. If out of the blue your grandchildren spontaneously start singing it you'll know they carry the recessive "*Padre benigno*" gene. The song gives thanks for the food we were about to receive, and we definitely were grateful for the daily rice and beans and even for the corned hash, but the warm powdered milk and the cooked *calabaza* were not my favorites. We couldn't go to the playground until we finished our lunch, and that *calabaza* cost me playtime more than once, even with Doña Venancia's coaxing. The glass of warm milk was our little daily trauma, repeatedly mentioned here, and we all had our coping strategies, but it was no doubt good for us, better than the lard-drenched *pegao*, which we loved.

Besides a square meal, the school took other measures to improve our health. We were periodically tested for lice and tropical parasites, and if parasites were detected the dreaded *purgante* loomed. Along with several of the other writers included in this collection, I was forced to down it on occasion. Warm powdered milk was golden nectar compared to that nasty potion, but it worked, I can assure you. Better the purge, however, than the dreaded *taenia* or tapeworm we learned about in health class. I still remember Dad taking us out of class to get the newly available polio vaccine. Polio was a scary word for our parents and one you don't hear much anymore, thank goodness. Some things have changed for the better.

Finally, after a few years there came a day when we donned our little caps and gowns and marched to the front of the Betania church in Pulguillas to the tune of "Pomp and Circumstance." On the front wall of the church was a large painting of the Good Shepherd, Jesus, with a lamb in his arms. Having learned a few facts and important lessons and negotiated the perils of primary and middle school education with the help of our good shepherds in Escuela Menonita Betania, we were ready to romp on our own, or so we thought.

Outside the comfort of our church and school spheres lurked a big, bad world that we couldn't always avoid. Hurricane Betsy or Santa Clara came barreling through in 1956 and flattened us for a time. Even more ominous loomed the Russian bear and his nuclear bombs. The fear was reinforced by the *simulacros* that happened from time to time. If we were in a car we pulled over to the side of the road and waited until the sirens stopped wailing. How we came to fear Russians, whom we had never seen, in the remote mountains of Puerto Rico is something that still makes me wonder, but the anxiety was real even as children. I had selected my hiding place if the apocalyptic event came to pass: Coamo Arriba. Surely nobody could find you or bomb you there. I'm glad to see from the stories here that others also shared my anxiety. On a lighter note, I don't recall the circus ever coming to Aibonito but the political caravans, with their loudspeakers blaring, were good for a little distraction.

What We Cherish and Value

Finally, the contributors to this book concur that the experience of growing up Mennonite in Puerto Rico is cherished and valued. All would likely agree with Carolyn Holderread's assessment that it was "the best gift my parents gave me." Some of the writers are grateful for advantages derived from living in another culture, learning another language, and broadening their world view.

Others value the opportunities derived from interacting with outsiders who came to live and serve among them. These opportunities included, for some, meeting the person who would become their life companion. In his contribution Rolando Santiago has shared his vivid love story. Others mention the lasting friendships they formed during these years, friendships that make it possible to come home again, in the words of Sherilyn Hershey Layne.

Several remark that the experiences of those years shaped them into what they became as adults. The benefits of a Christian education are noted and appreciated. Ruth Kaufman, for one, writes eloquently about the importance for her of the Christian heritage and foundation she was given in her formative years. Ted Springer, for his part, underscores the significance of having been part of an endeavor that brought about positive change.

Josian Rosario, Barbara Amstutz Hodel, and Dr. Weldon Troyer offer us a bridge to the early years of Mennonite work in Puerto Rico and remind us of the recognition owed the initiators and sustainers of this legacy, a legacy that lives on and is reflected in the faith and service of contributors Nilsa Pagán and Pastor José E. Jiménez Burgos. All contributors agree that their life would have been much different had the decisions taken at the crossroads mentioned by Rafo Falcón led someplace else.

French novelist Marcel Proust experienced a flood of childhood memories when he took a bite of a small sponge-cake dipped in tea. A bite of a curly, crunchy pig's tail roasted by contributor Juan A. Rolón would undoubtedly do the same for me.

ABOUT THE WRITERS

RAFAEL FALCÓN

Rafael was born and raised in Aibonito, Puerto Rico as part of the Ramón and Ana Luisa (Meléndez) Falcón family. He attended the Academia Menonita Betania from 1955 to 1962; studied at the Bonifacio Sánchez Jiménez High School in Aibonito, graduating in 1965; and in 1968 received his undergraduate degree in Spanish from the Inter-American University in San Germán. Rafael then did graduate studies at the University of Iowa, earning M.A. and Ph.D. degrees in 1977 and 1981. He was a Spanish professor at Goshen College for 32 years, and retired in 2011. Rafael lives in Goshen, Indiana with his wife Christine.

GALEN GREASER

Galen grew up in Puerto Rico as a member of the Lawrence and Annabelle (Troyer) Greaser household. He attended Betania and the Aibonito High School, and graduated from Inter-American University in San Germán in 1969. Galen obtained an M.A. degree in Latin American Studies at the University of Texas, and worked as a freelance translator for several years. He was then employed as the translator and curator of the Spanish Collection of the Texas General Land Office for several decades before retiring in 2011. Galen lives in Austin, Texas, with his wife Carmen Ramos.

CAROLYN HOLDERREAD HEGGEN

Carolyn, after graduating from Hesston College and Oregon State University, returned to Puerto Rico where she taught at Academia Menonita Betania for several years. She married Richard Heggen, and after moving to New Mexico where he joined the engineering faculty of the University of New Mexico, she completed her PhD and became part of the graduate Counseling faculty of Webster University. They spent a year in Pakistan with the Fulbright Foundation and two and one-half years in Nepal with Mennonite Central Committee (MCC). Currently they live in Corvallis, Oregon. Carolyn is a frequent international lecturer and consultant on trauma healing, gender issues, and human sexuality, and is co-developer and co-presenter of Sister Care International. She and Richard have three adult children, two grandchildren, and wonderful friends scattered around the world.

BARBARA AMSTUTZ HODEL

Barbara, the eldest of six children of H.Clair and Florence B. Amstutz, was raised in Goshen, Indiana during World War II. Her father fulfilled his obligation to the military draft as a physician in La Plata, Puerto Rico. After his first year there, his young family joined him, and her parents continued to serve with MCC for two more years. After returning to the States, Barbara was educated at Goshen public schools, Hesston (Kansas) Academy, and Goshen College, finishing with a degree in nursing. She married Paul E. Hodel in his senior year at Northwestern Medical School in Chicago, and subsequently lived wherever his specialty education in anesthesia required. Their service included two years in the Congo with MCC, twelve years in Harlan, Kentucky, and twenty-six years in Toledo, Ohio. During that time, Barbara volunteered in the communities in which they lived. She was occasionally called on to teach, preach, and write. Retired, they now have two children, five grandchildren, and pursue their interest in music and continued service in the Mennonite church in Goshen.

JOSÉ E. JIMÉNEZ BURGOS

José E. took his first communion in the Catholic church and enjoyed social activities with the Baptist church in his community. At age 15 he was baptized in the Mennonite Church. While a young man he participated with his pastor in a radio program called *La Hora de Reformación*, and served on the church council and taught Sunday School and Summer Bible School. José E. has participated on the board of directors for the Juventud Evangélica Menonita Puertorriqueña (JEMP) and the Concilio de las Iglesias Evangélicas Menonitas de Puerto Rico. Besides pastoring Mennonite congregations in Coamo and Cayey, other past employment has included positions as Secretario Ejecutivo de la Iglesia Menonita, and chaplain in the hospice program at the Hospital General Menonita in Aibonito. He has earned an M.A. in Religion at the Seminario Evangélico de Puerto Rico. José E. is currently the pastor of the Mennonite church in Aibonito, and director of Pastoral Care Program and Chaplaincy Services of the Mennonite Health System. He lives in Aibonito with his wife Vilma Rolón. They have three adult children.

SHERILYN HERSHEY LAYNE

Sherilyn was born May 4th, 1945 in Chicago, Illinois to missionary parents Lester and Alta Hershey. In April 1947 the Hershey family moved to Puerto Rico where they lived in La Plata, Pulguillas, Aibonito and in Llanos, a neighborhood close to Aibonito. During her 16 years in Puerto Rico, Sherilyn attended the Academia Menonita Betania, the Baptist Academy in Cayey and Aibonito High School. She then left the Island to attend Eastern Mennonite College in Harrisonburg, Virginia, where she graduated in 1967. She worked as a social worker for eight years in New York City, Charlottesville in Virginia, and West Liberty in Ohio. For the past 40 years Sherilyn has worked as a travel advisor in Richmond, Virginia, and continues to enjoy arranging cruise vacations. She has been married to Cliff Layne for 20 years and enjoys her family of two adult step-children and a granddaughter. Cliff and Sherilyn are active in the Hope Community Church of the Nazarene in Mechanicsville, Virginia, where she is involved with Women's Ministries.

NILSA PAGÁN ROSADO

Nilsa is from Aibonito, the "City of Flowers," in Puerto Rico. She studied at the Academia Menonita Betania from fourth to ninth grade, and graduated from the Dr. José N. Gándara High School. Nilsa served as a Sunday school teacher, on the church council, in the choir and other positions in the Iglesia Menonita of Aibonito. Currently she is retired, having moved to Tampa, Florida in 2014, after working for 27 years at Baxter Health Care Corporation in Aibonito. Her favorite pastimes are baking and cooking, and sharing with her family. At the moment Nilsa is also helping in different ministries of the church she is attending.

JUAN ANTONIO ROLÓN

Juan grew up in Puerto Rico and attended Academia Menonita Betania. During his I-W term he completed training to become a licensed practical nurse, and worked at Hospital General Menonita. While part of the Voluntary Service unit in Aibonito, he met his future wife Odette Leininger. They have spent most of their married life in Ohio. He retired from Fulton County Health Center after 40 years of employment. Juan and Odette live in Archbold, and attend West Clinton Mennonite Church.

JOSIAN ROSARIO

Josian was born in Palo Hincado, Barranquitas, the third son of a family of nine. His first contact with the Mennonite Church as a young boy led to his baptism at the age of 16. He has served the church in different areas such as Sunday School teacher, youth leader, deacon, a member of the board of trustees of Academia Menonita Betania, and a member of Concilio de Iglesias Evangélicas Menonitas de Puerto Rico. Josian studied at the Universidad Interamericana in San Germán, Puerto Rico and graduated with a B.A. in Spanish. Later he earned a master's degree from the Universidad de Puerto Rico. He worked as a Spanish teacher in his hometown high school for 15 years, and as Spanish supervisor in the Departamento de Educación Pública de Puerto Rico for an additional 15 years. He has been married to Áurea E. Menéndez for 40 years. They have two adult children and four grandchildren.

ROLANDO SANTIAGO

Rolando served in Puerto Rico as Bible teacher at Academia Menonita de Summit Hills from 1981–84, and edited the *Alcance Menonita*, a newsletter of the Convención de Iglesias Evangélicas Menonitas de Puerto Rico. In the United States, he was an evaluator of children's mental health services for the State of New York and for the federal Department of Health and Human Services in Maryland. He served twice with the Mennonite Central Committee U.S.: as assistant director from 1979–81 and as executive director, 2004–10. Rolando currently is executive director for the Lancaster Mennonite Historical Society, and lives with his spouse, Raquel Trinidad, in Lancaster, Pennsylvania.

TED SPRINGER

Ted was born in the Mennonite Hospital at its original site in La Plata. He attended the Academia Menonita Betania through ninth grade, and graduated from high school at Robinson School in Santurce, Puerto Rico. He attended Hesston College and Goshen College, where he graduated with a bachelor degree in Biology in 1972. In 1973 he began his career in medical diagnostics research and development at Miles Laboratories, Inc., later Bayer Corporation. The majority of his career involved product development, operations management, international manufacturing and strategic planning at large international medical diagnostics firms. In 2004, Ted joined HandyLab, Inc., a startup company, which successfully developed instruments and diagnostic reagents for the rapid detection of infectious diseases. After the sale of this company, he retired as VP of Manufacturing with BD Diagnostics in Ann Arbor, Michigan. Ted and his wife, Marlene Slagle, enjoy summers in Middlebury, Indiana and winters in Sarasota, Florida and visiting their two adult daughters and grandchildren. He enjoys golf, biking, fishing and the great outdoors, where he is still awed by the wonders of land and sea.

RUTH KAUFMAN STRUBE

Ruth was born in La Plata, Puerto Rico in 1956 to Provi Carrasquillo and Orvin Kaufman. She has two siblings: James and a twin sister Edith. She graduated from Wawasee High School in Syracuse, Indiana in 1975, and earned an Associate of Arts degree in Biblical Studies from the Christian Training Center in Fort Wayne, Indiana in 1979. Her work experience has included roles such as secretary for the Lester Sumrall Evangelistic Association, day care teacher, ownership of a residential cleaning business, and pastor's wife for 21 years. For the past 18 years, she has been a sales associate at Walmart. Ruth is married to Christopher Strube, and they reside in Ottumwa, Iowa. The couple has four adult children and two granddaughters.

WELDON TROYER

Weldon went to Puerto Rico in 1944 with his parents Dr. George and Kathryn Troyer. He attended high school at the Baptist Academy of Barranquitas from 1946 to 1949. His college education took place at Hesston College and Goshen College, where he graduated in 1953. That same year he returned to Puerto Rico where he worked as a laboratory technician at the La Plata Hospital in I-W service. From 1955 to 1959 he attended the University of Puerto Rico School of Medicine, and then completed his internship in Indianapolis, Indiana in 1960. Weldon practiced medicine in Goshen, Indiana, during which time he joined with three other physicians to create the Hyde Park Group. Under this organization, which had the goal of supporting one of the physicians at a time in a year of medical mission service, he worked from 1965-66 as a physician at the Aibonito Mennonite Hospital. Weldon retired in 2002. For eight years he was a board member of the Robert D. Ehret Good Samaritan Foundation, a philanthropic organization located in Puerto Rico. Weldon lives in Goshen, Indiana.

ABOUT THE EDITORS

RAFAEL FALCÓN was born in Aibonito, Puerto Rico. His parents, of Catholic tradition, began attending the La Plata Mennonite Church in 1955, and in that same year registered him as a third-grader in Academia Menonita Betania. After graduating from Betania as a ninth-grader and completing high school and college, he returned to Betania in 1968 to teach junior-high Spanish and Social Studies for two years. From 1973 to 1976 he served as the first Puerto Rican director of the school.

Falcón received his bachelor degree from the Interamerican University of Puerto Rico, and finished one year of graduate studies at the Universidad de Puerto Rico. He completed his master's and doctoral degrees in Spanish American Literature at the University of Iowa.

He has published books and articles on a variety of themes, including Puerto Rican immigration to the United States, Afro-Hispanic influence in literature, Hispanic culture, and Hispanic Mennonite history. In 1985 Herald Press published his *La Iglesia Menonita Hispana en Norte América: 1932-1982*, as well as its translated version. *Salsa: A Taste of Hispanic Culture* came out in 1998; a collection of short stories, *Mi Gente: In Search of the Hispanic Soul* in 2008; and *Historia del Menonitismo Hispanohablante: 1917-1990* in 2016. In addition, he edited textbooks for the teaching of Spanish as a Second Language, and has co-edited several works for the Colección Menohispana with collaborator Tom Lehman.

Falcón is a retired professor of Spanish language, Spanish American literature, and Hispanic culture from Goshen College, Goshen, Indiana, where he taught for 32 years.

Rafael and his wife, Christine Yoder, are the parents of two adult sons, Bryan Rafael and Brent Daniel, and the proud grandparents of Willow and Sebastian.

TOM LEHMAN was born in eastern Ohio, the son of school teachers who served in mission work for the Mennonite Church in Ethiopia and Puerto Rico.

He completed his undergraduate studies at Goshen College and obtained a graduate degree in Library Science from Indiana University. He retired from the University of Notre Dame Hesburgh Library after working there for 26 years, first as a cataloger, then as Digital Access Librarian.

He edited *MyLibrary Manual* in 2006 and co-edited *Making Library Web Sites Usable* in 2009. In 2013 he published Justus Holsinger's previously unpublished 1970 manuscript *Puerto Rico: Island of Progress*.

For the past nine years he has been digitizing missionary photos taken outside the United States in the mid-20th century. Photos from this collection have been the subject of two books and have appeared in numerous books, magazine articles, and TV shows, and are the source of many of the photos in the present publication. They can be seen at www.flickr.com/photos/telehman/.

He has collaborated with Rafael Falcón in the editing and publication of the books in the Colección Menohispana series.

Tom is married to Mary Windhorst and has three children, Jason, Kevin, and Jessica. He enjoys paddling and camping in wilderness areas and spending time with his five grandchildren.

PHOTO GALLERY

Children in line at Betania in front of school bus in the 1950s

Barbara Amstutz standing between her parents in this late 1940s farewell photo

Rolando Santiago in early 1960s with his little brother Ricardo and neighbors Becky and Betsy Rivera

Third and fourth graders with Betania teacher Patricia Brenneman in 1955. Students include Rafael Falcón in second row, extreme right; Galen Greaser standing next to him; Tom Lehman in third row, second on left; and Carolyn Holderread in back, extreme left

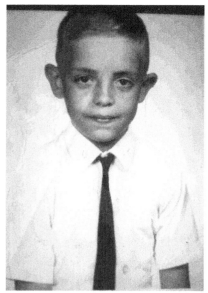

José E. Jiménez Burgos, nine years old, at his First Communion

Carolyn Holderread, in center with hair in braids, with Ulrich Foundation group in the 1950s

Galen Greaser, standing in back on right, in a 1960s family picture

Rafael Falcón, a Betania third grader in 1955, opening an MCC Christmas package

Nilsa Pagán Rosado as a 6th grader in Betania uniform in the 1969 yearbook

At a camp for university students, in back, Josian Rosario, second on left; Odette Leininger, center; and Juan Rolón, second on right

Palo Hincado church dedication in 1956

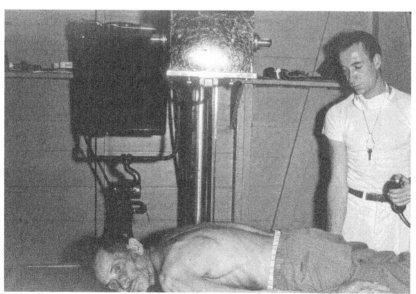

Weldon Troyer in X-ray room with patient in early 1950s

Ruth Kaufman in front row on right with her family in the early
1960s

Sherilyn Hershey, known as Chela to Island friends, pictured here in
front row on right with her family in the 1950s

Nursing graduation photo that triggered the love story of Raquel Trinidad and Rolando Santiago

Tom Lehman by the Betania comedor in the late 1950s

Casa Aibonito, home and headquarters for the Ulrich Foundation workers and activities

Ted Springer in back row, fifth from left, with Betania classmates and teacher Sr. Fernando L. Cains

Children enjoying tetherball, a favorite Betania activity for many years

Betania teachers, December 1955. From left: Carol Glick, Mercedes Meléndez, Patricia Santiago, Doris Snyder, Martha Kanagy, Anna K. Massanari, Marcelino Resto, Floyd Zehr, Allan Kanagy

Betania's famous "truck buses" of the 1950s

PHOTO CREDITS:

Children in line at Betania in front of school bus
Patricia Santiago photo in Tom Lehman collection
Barbara Amstutz as family is about to leave Puerto Rico
H. Clair Amstutz photo in Tom Lehman collection
Rolando and Ricardo Santiago with Becky and Betsy Rivera
Patricia Santiago photo in Tom Lehman collection
Third and fourth graders with Betania teacher Patricia Brenneman
Patricia Santiago photo in Tom Lehman collection
Carolyn Holderread with North American Ulrich Foundation families
Carolyn Holderread Heggen photo
José E. Jiménez Burgos in First Communion photo
José Jiménez photo
Rafael Falcón, third grade, opening MCC Christmas package
Gerald Wilson photo in Tom Lehman collection
Nilsa Pagán Rosado as Betania sixth grader
1969 Betania yearbook
Galen Greaser in a family photo
Lawrence Greaser photo in Tom Lehman collection
Josian Rosario and Juan Rolón at camp for university students
Martha Kanagy photo in Tom Lehman collection
Palo Hincado church dedication
Martha Kanagy photo in Tom Lehman collection
Weldon Troyer giving patient an X-ray
Jim Snyder photo in Tom Lehman collection
Ruth Kaufman in a family photo
John Lehman photo in Tom Lehman collection
Sherilyn Hershey in a family photo
John Lehman photo in Tom Lehman collection

Raquel Trinidad nursing graduation photo
Raquel Trinidad photo

Tom Lehman in front of Betania comedor
John Lehman photo in Tom Lehman collection

Casa Aibonito, Ulrich Foundation headquarters
Lawrence Greaser photo in Tom Lehman collection

Ted Springer in Sr. Cains' class photo at Betania
Leroy and Maxine Yoder photo in Tom Lehman collection

Children enjoying tetherball at Betania
Gerald Wilson photo in Tom Lehman collection

Betania teachers at newly planted palm tree
Patricia Santiago photo in Tom Lehman collection

Betania's "truck buses"
Martha Kanagy photo in Tom Lehman collection

Made in the USA
Monee, IL
01 June 2023

34668133R00105